Wisht Waters

WISHT WATERS
The Cult & Magic of Water

Gemma Gary

© 2017 Gemma Gary

First Published by Three Hands Press as:
Wisht Waters – Aqueous Magica & the Cult of Holy Wells

First Troy Books printing in paperback December 2022

ISBN 978-1-909602-55-7

All rights reserved.
No part of this publication may be reproduced, stored within a retrieval system or transmitted in any form or by any means, electronic, mechanical, photocopying, scanning, recording or otherwise, without the prior written permission of the author and the publisher.

Any practices or substances described within this publication are presented as items of interest. The author and the publisher accept no responsibility for any results arising from their enactment or use. Readers are self responsible for their actions.

Published by Troy Books
www.troybooks.co.uk

Troy Books Publishing
BM Box 8003
London WC1N 3XX

Cover design: Gemma Gary

Acknowledgements

With Grateful thanks to:
Jane Cox, Steve Patterson, The Museum of Witchcraft & Magic,
Daniel Schulke, Scarborough Museums Trust and to Ruchard
Puxley and Christine Gary.

Dedicated to Inky

Contents

Introduction	9
Chapter 1 - The Magic of Springs and Holy Wells	12
Chapter 2 - The Magic of Pools, Ponds and Lakes	80
Chapter 3 - The Magic of Flowing Waters	89
Chapter 4 - The Magic of the Sea	99
Chapter 5 - The Magic of Dew	110
Chapter 6 - Charm Waters	115
Chapter 7 - Methods of Hydromancy	131
Chapter 8 - Beings, Spirits and Deities	137
Chapter 9 - Water and the Witch Cult	157
Bibliography	*174*

Photoplates

Section 1 between pages 60-61
Section 2 between pages 120-121

All photography by Jane Cox

Introduction

Water fascinates; draws the eye and the mind into its depths, or into hypnosis via the mirrored world dancing upon its living surface. The voices of the sea-wave, stream and droplet returning to the cavern's pool, speak to the deeper self with utterances that seem as old as time itself. Unto the witch and occultist encountering the waters of the earth, a numinous window of otherworldly access opens; co-mingling in conflux the twin tributaries of Craft-stream and divine spirit-gnosis.

To our eyes the ancient rock exemplifies solidity and permanence, yet even it yields to the sculpting hand of water through the aeons, holding for us a sense of timelessness, the primordial, transformation and creation itself.

Around water has grown in humanity a myriad of belief; steeped in cult, ritual, magic and folklore. As will have been observed throughout the ages, throughout the world, the absence of water fast results in the absence of life, and with the return of water to the barren and parched earth, either welling forth from the depths, or falling from the heavens, the miraculous quickly occurs with the re-clothing of the land in verdancy and animate life. It is not surprising to us then that much of the beliefs surrounding water, in all of its manifestations, relate to its regenerative and transformative virtues – the ability to create change in all states from disease to health, from sterility to fertility, from ignorance to wisdom and even from death unto resurrection. Endowed with such miraculous potency and virtue, it is also of no surprise that the 'water cult in Britain', which may have its origins some five thousand years in our past,[1] is home to a host of spirits, divinities and otherworldly beings, which in congruence with the mysteries of life from death, creation from chaos, are often of a thoroughly dark and sinister nature.

We live in an age when many in the world are fortunate to enjoy the luxurious amenity of an unfailing piped water supply, and so for many water may have become an essential of life taken for granted, yet still it holds the power to fascinate. This power is exercised not only over the magically inclined, for bodies of water have the ability to become for most people a focal point for contemplation and inexplicable instinctual ritualistic behavior, alongside more conscious considerations of water as a recourse for healing and the fulfillment of wishes.

Behind such widespread contemporary reactions lies a long tradition of veneration and spiritual interaction and exchange with water and its otherworldly presences.

It is this tradition that is the focus of this brief discourse; in particular the operative folk-magical uses of water, such as for the purposes of healing, divination, fertility, protection and the lifting and placing of curses, each with their concomitant ritual acts. My approach will be via water's employment within popular magic, as well as within the Art Magical and its associations with the witch cult.

The traditions, lore and old magic of holy wells and springs, holy water, dew, the sea, rivers, streams, lakes and pools; as well as their divinities and spirits are herein to be explored. Naturally, my focus may revolve (particularly but not exclusively) around these

---

1. Bord, Janet and Colin. *Sacred Waters*, p.9.

Introduction

traditions as manifest in my current locale – the West Country of the British Isles, where the waters of such places might be described as 'Wisht'. This is a word to be encountered in the dialects of Devon, Cornwall and Somerset, describing the presence of supernatural influences, or all that is 'weird' or 'uncanny'.[2] Here, pale, weak or sickly people might be described as looking 'wisht'; as though they had been ill-wished. Times that are seen to be 'wisht', including dusk, dawn, midnight, May's Eve and Midsummer's Eve, for they are 'uncanny' times during which all acts of magic, divination or charming might be undertaken with greater potency or success.[3] The traditions explored herein though are by no means isolated nor unique to this region, but are given as examples whose likeness may be encountered within the cult, lore and traditions of water further afield and aboard.

---

2. Howard, Michael. *West Country Witches*, p. 202.
3. Caple, John, and Leyshon, Nell. *Somerset*, p. 30.

The Magic of Springs & Holy Wells

Leaving my Fellows for a while to the light and warmth of the Compass fire, I step into the dark and cold of night; tree-branch fingers tease back the anonymity of my hood and claw at my face and hair until, out and exposed in the moonlight, I disappear again beneath the earth. Sitting on the stone steps covered by the sodden mulch of the leaves of autumn past – their moisture seeping through the layers of humble garb to sting with cold at my skin – my eyes adjust to feast upon the splendour of the richest green mosses glowing with a strange luminosity in the flickering light of a solitary candle, and in the moonlight that filters past me from the opening above. Black, however, are the waters of the pool before me, appearing as though their depths know no end. As I drowse there and imbibe of the awakening virtue, a tangible mist in the verdant corbelled chamber wraps a soporific blanket about me and I have to reach out against the damp moss covered stones to steady myself from falling – or being drawn forward into the chill water... Mysterious knockings and tapings occur toward the back of the chamber – an activity of the native spirit folk, either to aid or confuse – I have company again!

Sancreed Well, or the Well of Chapel Downs, is perhaps my favourite in the West of Cornwall, and it is widely regarded as being the most mysterious. Certainly there are no known extant records of lore or tradition associated with the well, which was itself only rediscovered, overgrown and hidden, in 1879 by the Vicar of Sancreed. Yet, this mystery and lack of established tradition only gives rise to a useful sense of 'all-potential', there to be engaged with by the magically inclined visitor in this most ancient-feeling of wells, whose exact age and origins, like many of Cornwall's holy wells, are also shrouded in mystery. Experiences most often reported by visitors to this particular well tend to relate to its powerfully restful atmosphere, and sometimes trance, vision and sleep inducing virtue. The trance states and visions experienced at Sancreed Well, it has been suggested, might relate to high levels of radiation in the chamber; the water having been recorded as giving a radiation count 200% higher than background levels.[4]

Cornwall, it is said, is home to a higher number of extant holy wells than any other county in England.[5] Many of them are not the easiest of places to access,

---

4. Straffon, Cheryl. *Fentynyow Kernow*, p. 44.
5. Bord, Janet and Colin. *Cures and Curses – Ritual and Cult at Holy Wells*, p.154.

and may be found after negotiating treacherous deep-sucking bogs, or at the end of 'paths' long hidden beneath bracken, furze, blackthorn and brambles; tearing at clothing and at flesh. To visit such locations may indeed be a pilgrimage of dedication to a hidden, wild and lonely place where we may encounter the 'Other'.

When the locus of the holy well is reached, we find ourselves in a place of all-pervading presence; somehow cut off, or separate from the everyday world of men. Time may strangely seem to flow differently, and our thoughts may ponder a past when such places were a vital focal point within the community for ceremonies conducted around the curative and prescient waters.

Undoubtedly, with the sweeping hand of progress and agriculture's dominance of the landscape, many such places will have been lost, along with standing stones and circles of the ancients. Industrial progress, modernity and scientific enlightenment also, of course, set in motion a rapid decline in folk-magical belief and the common recourse to the spirit world to resolve life's difficulties. The medicaments increasingly available to the ordinary folk from doctor and chemist played the major role in drawing custom away from the well guardian, 'green-pharmacy' and witch alike.

The many holy wells that do though remain; some re-discovered and restored, some seeming to have been in continued use for centuries, have their regular visitors seeking to make some connection to the virtues of the waters, or the spirit of place, as exemplified by the variety of offerings to be seen today at nearly all such loci. Falling under the category today of 'sacred site', the holy wells may appear to more immediately inviting of deeper, perhaps instinctual, connection and interaction than the recondite menhir, circle and cromlech. Perhaps this is due to the fascination that water itself holds; for even where artificial pools and fountains appear, the deep-seated desire to make some votive interaction is quickly revealed via the rapid accumulation of immersed coin.

❧ Holy Wells and Dual-Faith ❧

Whilst a majority of the holy wells appear to have become associated with Christian Saints, or dedicated to their name, much of the lore and practice surrounding holy wells would seem to be of a decidedly pre-Christian 'pagan' character. Much of the folklore surrounding the Saints, and their wells, contain feats rather more reminiscent of the activities or powers of ancient pagan deities or spirits than early Christian pioneers.

Of course, the story of Christianity in Britain is not one of a clean-cut shift from the 'Old Ways' to the new religion; rather, it was a transition of concession on both sides with the pendulum of spiritual alignment amongst the people of Britain swinging to-and-fro a number of times between their native paganism and the incoming faith. As a result, there was no outright 'stamping out' of paganism, but Christianity in many cases absorbed pagan custom, tradition and belief, thus has paganism greatly influenced and changed the new religion as it settled in these lands. To this day, the seasonal customs and festivities of the British Christian calendar remain heavy with pagan influence, and our folk-magical traditions and practices are more often than not decidedly 'Christo-pagan' in nature. Perhaps nowhere is this more vividly exemplified than in the continuity of popular magical practice at holy wells.

The presiding spirit, or deity of the waters was superceded at many wells by a Christian saint or angel,[6] however, at such Christianised wells, the old spirit of place or pagan deity still survives, often veiled in 'faery

---

6. Howard, Michael. *By Standing Stone and Holy Well*, *The Cauldron* No. 137.

lore' and play an important role in the magical and divinatory ceremonies long conducted there. In some cases, the pagan spirit or deity of the well was preserved under a new identity, for whilst many of the well's saints are documented historical early Christian figures, others appear to be the original pagan spirit or deity reinvented under a new Christian guise.[7] For example, behind the Matron Saint of Ireland Brighid of Kildare we may find the goddess Brigid; both being associated with the tending of sacred fires and the festivities of February the 1st. Likewise it is suggested that holy wells dedicated to St Helen/Elen may have originally been associated with the Celtic water goddess Alauna.[8] The cult of the Blessed Virgin Mary allowed an ancient pagan reverence for the divine feminine to continue, albeit veiled beneath the Church's denial of female sexual potency, and it is quite possible that many of the holy wells dedicated to the Virgin Mary, may have been associated with female divinity, or the Mother Goddess.

The Sacred Head and the Creative Act

Centrally emblematic to the cult of the holy well is the human head, believed cross-culturally to be a seat of the soul, thus strongly associated with the divine, inspiration and the utterance of the word of creation.

The cultic significance of the head may be traced through to the Iron Age peoples of the British isles; collectors of the skulls of those they defeated in battle, and further back still through the peoples of the Bronze and Neolithic Ages.[9] To the ancient peoples of the

---

7. Bord, Janet and Colin. *Sacred Waters*, p. 35.
8. Howard, Michael. *By Standing Stone and Holy Well*, The Cauldron No. 137.
9. Howard, Michael. *Welsh Witches and Wizards*, p. 140-141.

British Isles, the head appears to have represented a sacred vessel of the soul, the very potency of life itself and the power of the divine.[10]

As a fetish of power, to the ancient 'head-hunting' cultures, the captured heads of their enemies may have represented the 'capturing' also of their soul,[11] wisdom and vitality, perhaps seen to bring an increase to the captor's own skills and strength in battle.

The collected heads placed on display at the entrances to fortified homesteads may also have served a protective function; both of an occult nature in the warding of harmful supernatural agencies, or against potential enemies of a corporeal nature.[12] Perhaps here we have an explanation for the Celts' prolific use of the head in ornamentation, possibly as a magical device of empowerment and protection.

The Celtic cult of the sacred head survived and adapted through the arrival and spread of Christianity, eventually to become heavily associated with the cults of the saints and the sacred springs and wells.

Within the folklore of holy wells and sacred springs in the British Isles, there exist numerous 'well-creation myths' featuring the miraculous powers possessed by the decapitated heads of the Christian Saints. These legends follow a common thread, in which the sacred waters mysteriously arise from the depths of the earth at the very spot where the severed head of the saint falls.[13] Given the commonality of the theme, a few examples should here suffice.

In Devonshire's Exeter, the virgin Saint Sidwell, or Sativola, was decapitated whilst at prayer by reapers using a

---

10. Ibid, and Bord. Janet and Colin, *Sacred Waters*, p. 16.
11. Whelan, Edna. *The Magic and Mystery of Holy Wells*, p. 44-45.
12. Howard, Michael. *Welsh Witches and Wizards*, p. 140-141.
13. Bord, Janet. *Cures and Curses – Ritual and Cult at Holy Wells*, p. 61.

scythe. The murder, carried out upon the orders of her stepmother, resulted in a curative spring welling up from the spot where Sidwell's head fell. The spring became a holy well, once located on the site of the Church of St Sidwell, and was resorted to for its reputed healing powers.

Saint Sidwell

A particularly famous legend of well-creation by decapitation is perhaps that belonging to St Winefride's Well – 'the Lourdes of Wales' – in Holywell, Flintshire. The folklore of this holy well; an important healing and pilgrimage site since the 7th century, tells of its creation when Winefride; the beautiful virgin daughter of the King of Powys, was decapitated by Prince Caradoc ap Alyn who desired her in marriage.[14] Winefride, who had dedicated her life to Christ, rejected the advances of the prince, until, enraged, he drew his sword and beheaded her. St Beuno, rejoined his niece's severed head to her body and she was restored to life. St Beuno invoked a curse upon Caradoc, and he fell dead in an instant. The blood-stained earth, where Winefride's head fell erupted into a healing spring, and to this day pilgrims visit the site's elaborate well house and bathing pool to partake of the water's virtues.

Such was the continued faith in the spiritual potency of the head, particularly of a holy person, extant springs and wells might be sanctified by its virtue. Upon the murder of St Thomas Becket in Canterbury Cathedral in 1170, it is said that his blood and brains, spilled in the violent attack, were put into the waters of the well housed in the building. As a result, the waters of the well became a holy relic and were referred to as St Thomas's Blood.[15] Holy relics of all kinds were highly sought after in popular magic for the curative, and sometimes protective virtues they were believed to possess.

A major feature of the iconography of holy wells and fountains is the carved stone head. Part of the fabric of a number of holy wells, the stone head was sometimes incorporated into the well's rites, whilst others form a fount through the open mouth of which the virtuous water flows forth into the well-basin, being reminiscent

---

14. Howard, Michael. *Welsh Witches and Wizards*, p. 142-143
15. Bord, Janet and Colin. *Cures and Curses – Ritual and Cult at Holy Wells*, p. 5.

of the power of the Word of Creation. Other heads have no known traditions attached to them and are a mystery in itself. At the back of the beautiful well-house of St Anne's Well, Whitstone, North Cornwall, is an enigmatic carved stone head, startlingly primitive and 'pagan' in its beauty. Certainly, it has been suggested that this head may be pagan in origin, and a possible representation of the Goddess Anu.[16] St Tecla's, a holy well at Llandegla, Clwyd, with a tradition of complex healing ceremonies, was once home to six stone heads, which may have had a role in the rites that once took place there in the distant past. These heads are now said to be in the possession of a family local to the well.[17] The skulls and severed heads of humans appear also to have been incorporated into holy wells. Alongside a carved stone head, a real severed human head had been placed within a 3rd century well in Northwood, Hertford, whilst behind the lining of a 1st century well in Odell, Bedford, a human skull was discovered which had been purposefully installed there during its construction.[18] Such is the association of the head cult with the cult of sacred waters, that the image of the head was enthusiastically carried forward into the ornamentation of Christian fonts.[19] Some of the carved heads featured on fonts are remarkably 'pagan' in appearance, particularly those upon the font of the 12th century Church of St Germoe, Germoe, Cornwall. The font itself is believed the long predate the church building that houses it.

In Shropshire is an example of a holy well where a stone head formed a central role within its rites. At the back of the holy well of St Oswald, Oswestry, is a

---

16. Straffon, Cheryl. *Pagan Cornwall – Land of the Goddess*, p. 52.
17. Howard, Michael. *Welsh Witches and Wizards*, p. 138-139.
18. Bord, Janet and Colin. *Cures and Curses – Ritual and Cult at Holy Wells*, p. 123.
19. Bord, Janet and Colin. *Sacred Waters*, p. 20.

carved crowned head. The well was believed to have the power to grant wishes via a certain ritual which was to be performed at midnight. There, the wisher would take up water from the well in their hand and drink a little of it whilst making their wish. The remainder of the water then had to be cast over the carved stone head.[20]

There are numerous holy wells, even well into recent times, that have magical healing traditions involving the ritual use of human skulls. This is a tradition, surviving and adapted into modern era Christian usage from ancient pagan practice.[21] The tradition at these wells, of drinking the curative waters from the interior of a human skull, would suggest that from the skull itself are imparted into the waters additional virtues, perhaps associated with life force, divinity and creation. Perhaps by such practices, the sacred, curative waters were believed to be enhanced and given extra potency by the virtues associated with the sacred cultic vessel of the skull/head.

The ritual use of human skulls at holy wells is a tradition that appears to have been at its strongest in Wales but is not an isolated one, for it is found also in examples of well tradition in Ireland and Scotland.[22]

In Pembroke, West Wales, is perhaps the most widely renowned tradition of a skull's ritual use at a holy well which survived well into the 19th century. St Teilo's Well was home to a healing tradition using the skull of the 6th century Bishop St Teilo of Wales, which was in the guardianship of the Melchior family who lived close to the well. Those seeking a cure had to receive and drink the waters, handed to them in the skull of St Teilo by a member of the Melchior family who had to have been born in the family home in order for the rite to be

---

20. Bord, Janet and Colin. *Cures and Curses – Ritual and Cult at Holy Wells*, p. 63.
21. Howard, Michael. *Welsh Witches and Wizards*, p. 144.
22. Bord, Janet and Colin. *Sacred Waters*, p. 18.

successful. Another Welsh well at which water was drunk from a human skull for healing purposes was Ffynnon Llandyfaen in Carmarthenshire. Here the practice was still extant by 1815.[23]

The skulls employed in such rites were not always those associated with Christian saints or holy people. In Wester Ross in the North West Scottish Highlands, is the well of Tobar A' Chinn – meaning *The Well of the Head*.[24] Here, the skull employed within the well's curative rites was believed to have been that of a woman who had committed suicide in the 18th or 19th century. As a suicide, the woman was buried outside the churchyard, later however, her skull is said to have appeared on the surface of the ground, indicating that it was possessed of miraculous powers. The skull was taken to the well, where it was housed in a stone container. Sufferers of epilepsy would resort to the well in search of a cure. There they would be instructed by the guardian of the well in the ritual procedure that was to be performed. This rite involved the circumambulation of the patient around the well in the direction of the sun three times. The well guardian would then draw water from the well in the skull from which the patient had to drink three times.

A particularly macabre skull ritual was performed on the Isle of Lewis. Here a cure for epilepsy might be performed by a skull being disinterred from a graveyard at midnight and brought to the home of the patient who then would drink water from it drawn from a holy well. The ritual was completed by the skull's return to the graveyard for re-interment.[25]

---

23. Howard, Michael. *Welsh Witches and Wizards*, p. 144.
24. Bord, Janet and Colin. *Cures and Curses – Ritual and Cult at Holy Wells*, p. 125.
25. *Ibid.*

The Magic of Springs & Holy Wells

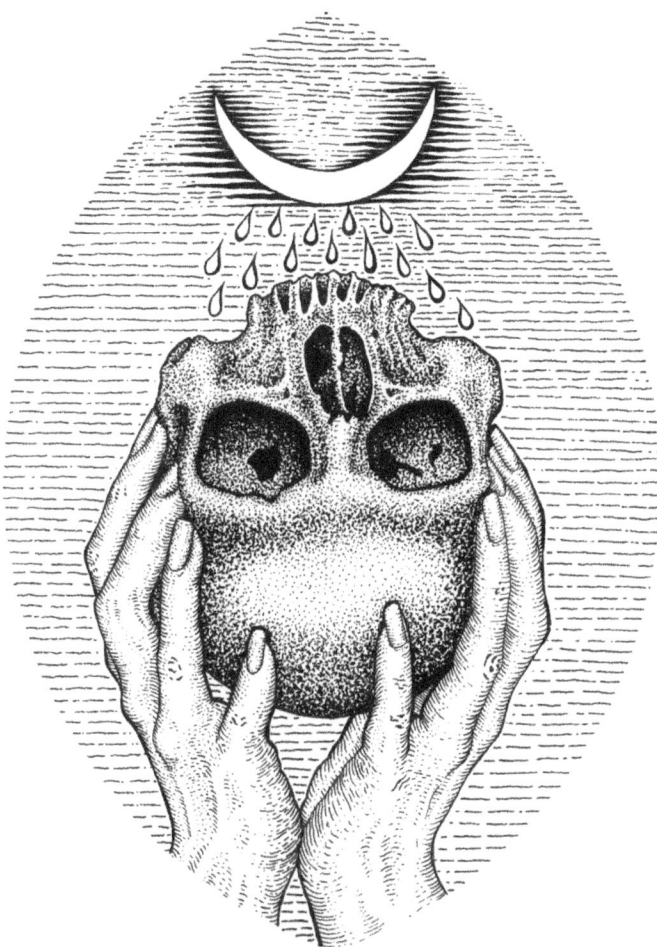

The use of water in which saintly relics have been steeped for curative or protective purposes is an established tradition within folk magic, thus water did not always have to be drunk directly from a skull in order for the patient to partake of the virtues of the osseous vessel. In Aberdeenshire, in the parish of Marnoch, Banff, water in which the skull of St Marnoch had been washed was considered for many years a potent curative for the sick.[26]

---

26. Bord, Janet and Colin. Sacred Waters, p. 19.

One possibility for the close relationship between the cult of the head and the water cult is the potency/fertility/phallic significance of head's symbolism. This places the head firmly within an arcane corpus of symbolism, tradition and lore surrounding the theme of 'the creative act' relative to holy wells, in which the proximity of the phallic symbol to the feminine waters could, in conjunction, be seen to be alchemically generative of the virtues given unto the waters of life. It is the waters of life which, in the cosmogonical myths of many ancient cultures, are the progenitrix of creation.[27]

It is perhaps this regenerative, creative power of water that has placed the holy well at the centre of healing traditions and baptismal rites. In healing, the sacred waters give the ailing rebirth unto a new life of renewed health.

The falling to earth of the severed head of virtue may be seen to have strong connotations of phallic fertility in the creation myths of holy wells. So too may the presence of carved stone heads above or within the well waters, the interment of an actual human head in the construction of wells and the employment of the human skull in imparting the well water's curative virtues.

Other common features with possible phallic symbolism in the presence of the feminine waters of holy wells include standing stones and trees.[28] As we shall see, such features often held central roles in the rites performed at wells. The sacred hawthorn, redolent with 'faery lore', is often to be found arching over a holy well, festooned with votive rags called 'clouties'. Here is a ritual practice in which the rag, representative of the ailment, is dipped in the curative well and affixed to the branches of the tree – a conjunction of

---

27. Courtney, R.A. Cornwall's Holy Wells – Their Pagan Origins, p. 3.
28. *Ibid*, p. 21.

the feminine waters and the masculine thorn to give creative potency unto the spell of rebirth from ailment unto health.

Other trees of significance located at well sites include the ash, elder, hazel, holly, oak, rowan and yew. In Ireland such trees are given the name 'bile'.[29]

The yew tree, renowned for its ancient associations with longevity and self-regeneration via its manner of growth, provides us with evidence that trees of significance at well sites were believed vital to the continued potency and virtues of the waters. A 'Well of the Yew Tree' in Easter Rarichie, Ross and Cromarty, had the power to cure the 'white swelling'. However, this power was dependant upon the continued presence of the site's yew tree, and when it was felled, the curative powers of the waters left the well.[30]

The Hazel tree, associated with the virtues of wisdom, inspiration, vision and protection, is, in Celtic tradition, heavily associated with sacred wells and springs.[31]

Irish mythology is home to various legends of a sacred 'Well of Knowledge', from which seven rivers flow forth, and is said to be the source of the rivers Shannon and Boyne. Some traditions name it Connla's Well and place it in Tipperary, others, the Well of Segais in the Otherworld. About this sacred well, nine Hazel trees are said to grow, and the nuts that fall from their branches into the well's waters, impart the powers of knowledge and seership unto the waters and to the 'Salmon of Knowledge' who feed upon them. Those who drink of the waters, or eat the salmon, receive the gifts of the nine hazels.[32]

---

29. Bord, Janet and Colin. *Cures and Curses – Ritual and Cult at Holy Wells*, p. 129.

30. Bord, Janet and Colin. *Sacred Waters*, p. 59.

31. *Ibid*, p. 13.

32. Bord, Janet and Colin. *Cures and Curses – Ritual and Cult at Holy Wells*, p. 129, & Whelan, Edna. *The Magic and Mystery of Holy Wells*, p. 102.

The sacred Salmon of Knowledge may itself be symbolic of phallic potency, fertility and generative 'life-force'. In Celtic belief, the salmon may also have represented underworld/chthonic divinity.[33]

The life-regenerative powers of the sacred fish of the well appear in Cornish legend. St Neot was told by an angel that within his well there lived three sacred fish, and if he removed only one each day to eat, the well's population of three would remain miraculously constant. The saint's servant however, when Neot was one day taken ill, took instead two of the fish from the well and cooked them for him. Upon realising this had happened, Saint Neot ordered his servant to return both of the fish to the well, whereupon both were miraculously revived unto life.

The tradition of the sacred fish of the well is not isolated to myth and legend, for such fish were present in actuality in holy wells where they were central to the wells' rites. Holy wells were inhabited by sacred fish until relatively recently.[34]

The late survival of the tradition of sacred fish present in holy wells seems to have been particularly strong in Wales. Two sacred fish lived in the Caernarfon well, Ffynnon y Sant, where they held a divinatory role within the curative rites regularly carried out there well into the 20th century.[35] Those seeking a cure would either bathe the afflicted limb in the well, or drink of its waters. After doing so, if the fish made themselves visible to the patient, a cure was foretold, if however they remained hidden in its depths, the ailment would remain.

Sacred fish dwelt in holy wells on Anglsey where they too performed divinatory roles, such as at the well of

---

33. Bord, Janet and Colin. *Sacred Waters*, p. 144.
34. *Ibid.*
35. *Ibid*, p. 146.

Ffynnon Bryn Fendigaid, and at Ffynnon Fair, where young people would watch for predictions regarding matters of love via the movements of the well's fish.[36]

As well as the tradition of the sacred head, the presence of standing stones, special trees and sacred fish, the theme of fertility and the creative conjunction of the masculine and the feminine may also be engendered by the situation and nature of a well itself. At the strange and brooding site of Roche Rock, a one time hermitage of St Conan and chapel dedicated to Saint Michael is perched high upon the eerie granite rock formations. Below, at its foot, a well is said to exist, strangely ebbing and flowing with the tide. Here we may perceive a creative conjunction of solar and lunar influences.[37]

The theme of the creative act can be seen also in the time of year most heavily associated in tradition with the potency of holy wells – the month of May. The May, summer's opening, redolent with themes of sexual fecundity, increase and the burgeoning of life, is, as we shall see, a time when many wells were seen to be at their most potent, and were visited in order to partake of their increased virtue, particularly in the healing of children. Even the widespread common act of dropping pins into holy wells as part of curative, divinatory and wishing rites, may, in its own way be symbolic of the power of the sexual creative act.

Like those involving the sacred head, the conjunction of the phallic and the feminine is symbolically alluded to in other well-creation myths involving the staff of a saint. Just like the well-creation myths involving the human head, those involving the staff are widespread and vary little in essential detail. Here, where a saint thrusts their staff into the earth, or strikes the earth, the virtuous chthonic waters spring forth and a holy well is

---

36. *Ibid.*
37. Straffon, Cheryl. *Fentynyow Kernow*, p. 31.

created. Examples from Cornwall include the creation of Jesus well at St Minver, where an unidentified traveling saint grew thirsty and thrust his staff into the parched sand dunes whereupon the sacred waters sprang forth.

The saintly staff and the sacred head are present both in the story of Saint Gwinear. The saint, who had come to Cornwall from Ireland was beheaded by a local king. Gwinear is said to have picked up his own head before striking his staff to the earth, causing waters to spring forth, in order to bathe it.
The theme of waters brought forth by the staff of a holy person is an old one and may of course have their antecedence in the bringing forth of waters by Moses for the Israelites upon Mount Horeb:

And Moses cried unto the LORD, saying, What shall I do unto this people? they be almost ready to stone me. And the LORD said unto Moses, Go on before the people, and take with thee of the elders of Israel; and thy rod, wherewith thou smotest the river, take in thine hand, and go. Behold, I will stand before thee there upon the rock in Horeb; and thou shalt smite the rock, and there shall come water out of it, that the people may drink. And Moses did so in the sight of the elders of Israel. Exodus 17:4-6

In closing our look at the theme of the creative act and the relationship between the sacred waters and staves of power, I would like to repeat a wonderful story of a modern West Country cunning man, related to Michael Howard by Paul Broadhurst. During the launch of Broadhurst's 'Secret Shrines', which took place at a Cornish Holy Well, Cecil Williamson (1909 – 1999), traditional magician and founder of the Museum of Witchcraft, was in attendance, bearing a heavy staff topped with an iron cross. Upon enquiring about the strange looking object, Cecil explained to Broadhurst that he had used it to perform a rite at the well in order to "bring back the Dragon banished by the Christians".

This he did by heating the iron cross with a blowtorch until it was glowing red hot before plunging it into the well waters, causing them to hiss and spit like a serpent.[38]

Wells, Witches & Guardians

That there exists a relationship between witch and well is exemplified by the many wells bearing the word witch in their name. This seems to be particularly so in Wales, where 'gwrach' meaning 'witch' gives names unto wells including Ffynnon y Wrach, Montgomeryshire, Ffrwd y Wrach in Cardiganshire, Rhdy Wrach in Carmarthenshire and Lyn Gwradiod in Pembrokeshire.[39]

Witches sometimes made their home near holy wells. Alsia Well, in Cornwall's West Penwith, we are told by William Bottrell was home to a widely reputed witch. She kept a garden well stocked with herbs from which she would prepare curative ointments and lotions, and was consulted for her healing abilities. She created and supplied magical charms and could lift the influence of 'black witchcraft' and the evil-eye as well as read people's fortunes. Her cottage, a little above Alsia Mill became a granary in the 1870's, but is again a home and is inhabited by Alsia's current well-guardian – Trevor Rogers.[40]

In Cornish tradition, we also find the ghost of a witch associated with a well. Two tin miners and their sister lived together in a small cottage close to a beautiful well near Kenidzhek. The two brothers gave their sister strict instructions that she was not to go near the well after daylight hours, but would give her no reason. One day however, upon forgetting to draw the next day's water,

---

38. Howard, Michael. *The Cunning Man*, *The Cauldron* No.95.
39. Howard, Michael. *Welsh Witches and Wizards*, p. 137-138.
40. Trevor Rogers has sadly passed away since the first publication of this book

she ignored her brother's warnings and made her way to the well after nightfall. As she approached the well, she noticed an elderly woman, wrapped about with a red shawl, crouching strangely in a break in the hedge. She spoke politely to the woman but received no response, and so set about drawing water from the well. However, although the pitcher she used was perfectly sound, and she saw it fill with water, each time she lifted the vessel from the well it would be empty. Becoming frightened, she made quickly for home whereupon meeting her brothers she told them of what had occurred. From them she discovered that the old woman she had seen was the reason why they wished her not to visit the well after daylight – for what she had seen was the ghost of 'Old Moll'; a black witch who had terrorized the community in her life and they saw her spirit, sat in the hedge by the well each night as they returned home from the mine.

It has been suggested that the well guardian, a figure once common at many holy wells, who would not only tend to the well, keeping it and its path clear, but would also instruct visitors in the traditions of the well, or in some cases play an important role in performing and overseeing its rites. It has been suggested that such well guardians may have formed some kind of survival of an ancient priesthood of the well cult.[41] As unlikely as this may seem, well guardians have been known to claim that it was only they who had the special ability to interpret the signs of the well in its associated rites of divination.[42]

As we shall see, a 19th century guardian of Madron well, Cornwall, was regarded as a wise-woman, supervising and instructing visitors and patients in the proper ritual procedure to be carried out at the well.

Also in Cornwall, not far from Madron, a well in Gulval had another wise-woman guardian in the 18th

---

41. Bord, Janet and Colin. *Cures and Curses – Ritual and Cult at Holy Wells*, p. 59.
42. *Ibid*, p. 151.

century, who cared for the well, and instructed visitors in its divinatory powers and was regarded at the time as a priestess of the well's virtues.

In Wales, a well named Ffynon Sarah in Caerwys, was cared for by a witch who gave the well its name. Like Gulval Well's wise-woman, Sarah was seen to hold a priestess-like role, for it was believed that the waters of the well would be of no beneficial use without her assistance.[43]

Traditionally, some wells were said to be the meeting place for witches' covens. Upon May's Eve and at Midsummer, witches were said to gather and dance at Skimmington Well in Somerset.[44]

A 'Witches Well' in the Quantocks was also said to be a meeting site for witches. Due to its association with witchcraft, a Cunning Man was called in to exorcise the well for farmers were too afraid to take their cattle there to drink. A ritual was performed in which the man said some 'special words' and cast salt into the well to rid it of evil. A ring of protective ash trees were also planted around the well.[45]

In the 17th century, a reputed witch lived in a small cottage beside a well in Irongray, Kirkcudbright, Scotland. She was said to perform rites by circumambulating widdershins around the well, which made others afraid to draw water for they believed, by her rites, some ill-influence had been imparted upon it. For this she was put to death by being rolled downhill in a blazing tar-barrel.[46]

In the West of Cornwall, modern day meetings of witch covens and other magical groups still take place at holy wells, particularly Madron well and its baptistery

---

43. Whelan, Edna. *The Magic and Mystery of Holy Wells*, p. 26.
44. Bord, Janet and Colin. *Sacred Waters*, p. 141.
45. Bord, Janet and Colin. *Cures and Curses – Ritual and Cult at Holy Wells*, p. 150.
46. Bord, Janet and Colin. *Sacred Waters*, p. 81.

chapel, Sancreed Well and Alsia Well. The current well-guardian of Alsia, Trevor Rogers, has observed folk making their way to the well silently, late at night, and has often found evidence of ritual having taken place there. He told this writer that, on one occasion, he discovered shards of smashed pottery lying about the place in a hidden grove beside the well which appeared to be the result of some kind of ceremony or magical working. The next morning, all trace of them had mysteriously disappeared.

Spirits of the Well

Like witches, the faery folk also gave their name to wells. In Cornwall such wells include the **Fairy Well** in Carbis Bay, used for making wishes, and at Blisland there is a **Fairies' Well**, the field next to which is said to be cursed if it is ever put to arable use and is kept to graze livestock. Also in Cornwall there is a **Piskies' Well** in Pelynt and near the Men an Tol stones is **Fenton Bebibell**, meaning 'well of the little people'. There was a tradition at this well of children blessing their dolls in the waters of this well; a custom that has recently been revived although the 'children' are now often a little older!

In Somerset, which is said to have been home to some ten fairy wells,[47] there is a **Pixy Well** near Cothelstone, and England is home to a number of wells bearing Puck's name.[48]

The blessing of the spirits of the well could be gained by making offerings or gifts of such things as pins, pebbles, white quartz stones, buttons, and coins or by hanging rags in the trees overhanging the well. A well at Minchmoor, Peebles, is called the **Cheese Well**; so named

---

47. Bord, Janet and Colin. *Cures and Curses – Ritual and Cult at Holy Wells*, p. 43.
48. *Ibid*, p. 44.

for the bits of cheese which were dropped into its water as a gift for its indwelling spirits.[49]

The Piskies' Well, Pelynt, also called St Nun's Well, was visited to gain the blessing of the piskies by making offerings of pins. It was believed that, by making an offering to the piskies of the well, one would be protected from the frightening experience of being pisky-led, as well as being granted good health, and good fortune in the husbandry of animals and crops.

Well spirits, like others, have their dark side and are not always beneficent in nature, thus the purpose of offerings was sometimes to guard against or reverse the harm that the spirit could cause. The spirit guardian of Cornwall's St Nun's Well, Pelynt, would bring misfortune upon the irreverent who failed to make an offering during a visit. Such people would also be haunted by the spirits of the dead in the form of moths.[50]

Inverness women who believed they had a changeling baby, would visit Fuaran a Chreigain to make an offering, such as a bowl of milk, and leave the changeling there overnight in the hopes that the fairies would exchange it for the human child by morning.[51]

The water of holy wells could be employed in various ways to provide protection against the faery folk. Pixy-led travelers on Dartmoor could break the spell by turning their cloaks and drinking from Fitz's Well. Two Dartmoor wells carry this name and the same pixy lore – one in Princetown, the other near Okehampton, both having been given enclosures by John Fitz, grandfather of Lady Howard and friend of Sir Frances Drake; a figure also associated with magical water lore.[52]

---

49. Bord, Janet and Colin. *Sacred Waters*, p. 137.
50. Straffon, Cheryl. *Fentynyow Kernow*, p. 25.
51. Bord, Janet and Colin. *Sacred Waters*, p. 137.
52. St. Leger-Gordon, Ruth E. *The Witchcraft and Folklore of Dartmoor*, p. 19-20.

According to traditional witch Roy Bowers/Robert Cochrane, in the Cotswolds an iron horseshoe nail that had been dipped in the waters of a spring formed a powerful charm to protect against the mischief of the 'little people'.[53]

When oatmeal cakes were put out to dry in Scotland, they might be sprinkled with water from a holy well in order to prevent spirits from consuming their etheric substance.[54]

In the 18th century, a magician was brought in to exorcise a well at Cresswell in south Pembrokeshire, for it was reputedly haunted by spirits in the form of 'White Ladies', causing the local people to avoid visiting the well after dark for fear of encountering the apparitions. To banish the spirits, the magician carved pentagrams into the trunks of beech trees growing near the well. One such pentagram was still visible on one of the trees around one hundred years ago.[55]

Exorcisms of evil spirits might be conducted in Powys by sealing the spirit into a bottle, which was then to be dropped into a well – water has a long use within magical tradition for spirit-binding.

At some wells, such as one near St Lawrence, Pembroke, the indwelling spirit was said to be the Devil himself.[56]

The Frog Well of Acton Burnell, Shropshire, lies near The Devil's Causeway and is said always to be inhabited by three frogs. The largest of the three is said to be the Devil accompanied by two of his imps.

A well named Holy Well, in Atwick, Yorkshire, is haunted by the dark and hooded figure of a one-eyed

---

53. Glass, Justine. Witchcraft, *The Sixth Sense – And Us*, p. 144.
54. Bord, Janet and Colin. *Sacred Waters*, p. 110.
55. Howard, Michael. *Welsh Witches and Wizards*, p. 129-130.
56. Bord, Janet and Colin. *Sacred Waters*, p. 148.

man, and close-by, the apparition of a headless horseman rides by.[57] The well's ghost has been likened to Woden, having much in familiarity with the Devil, both figures having close associations with the Wild Hunt and the role of the psychopomp.

❧ Patterns of Practice & Popular Magic ☙

Within the popular magic of holy wells, there are a variety of common patterns of practice that were observed with regard to ritual actions, offerings, and careful timing in accordance with tides of potency. The making of offerings of some kind is a practice common to many holy wells, particularly those associated with curative or divinatory traditions.

That the making of offerings to streams, rivers, wells, pools and of course bogs – liminal places in a state betwixt land and water, is an ancient practice is well known. That water was seen as a liminal portal between the world of the living and the world of spirit or the 'Other' is perhaps exemplified by the depositions of precious and finely crafted metal items sacrificed unto water from the late Bronze Age onwards unto recent times.[58]

It is very tempting indeed to see a link between the ancient sacrificing of metal objects unto the other world, via water, by first breaking or bending them, thus placing them beyond usefulness to the every-day world of man, with the popular practice of bending metal pins before dropping them into holy wells. Certainly, the one time practice of bending coins given to the Church, setting them aside from normal usage and marked out for the spiritual, seems to

---

57. Whelan, Edna. *The Magic and Mystery of Holy Wells*, p. 99.
58. Bord, Janet and Colin. *Sacred Waters*, p. 13-14.

follow this theme.[59] Whilst via folk-memory or instinctual behaviour, some form of ancient continuity may be represented, there are other, possibly parallel explanations in the folk magical association between crooked objects and good luck or protection such as the 'crooked sixpence'.[60] Pins, a common addition to protective 'witch-bottles' were sometimes bent. As, in folk-magical belief, magic and spirits were thought to travel in straight lines, a rich corpus of folk-magical protections involving the tangled, the twisted and the crooked to trap and confuse negative spiritual influences has evolved. It is possible that the bent pin, dropped into the well, could relate to the turning aside, or averting of harmful influences in operations of healing, wishing, or divination.

In curative well magic, we find pins used for the charming of warts. At some wells, pins would be stuck into each wart before being bent and thrown into the well, such as at St Baglan's Well, Llanfaglan and at Ffynnon Gynhafal, Denbigh.[61] One method calls for the finding, whilst walking to the well, of sheep wool. At the well, each wart was to be stuck with a pin before being rubbed with the wool. The pin was to be bent and thrown into the well, and then the wool impaled upon a spike of a nearby hawthorn. As the wool was scattered by the wind, so the wart would go.[62]

In divinatory practices, the throwing of pins into the well water would cause such things as bubbles to arise, their appearance, or number having some significance in the reading. At other wells the pin might cause a vision to materialise in the water's surface.[63]

---

59. Whelan, Edna. *The Magic and Mystery of Holy Wells*, p. 76.
60. Bord, Janet and Colin. *Cures and Curses – Ritual and Cult at Holy Wells*, p. 95.
61. *Ibid*.
62. *Ibid*, p. 140.
63. Whelan, Edna. *The Magic and Mystery of Holy Wells*, p. 77.

The Magic of Springs & Holy Wells

Other token offerings traditional at holy wells include such things as flowers, blackthorn spikes, buckles, buttons and stones. Pebbles of white quartz have been noted offerings at wells on the Isle of Man and in Wales. As previously mentioned, broken china has been discovered, possibly in relation to a magical working, at Alsia Well in Cornwall, so it is interesting to find that offerings of china pieces were made in Ireland at St Luctigern's Well at Fenloe.[64]

Next to pins, rags called 'clouties' where perhaps a most common form of well offering. Certainly today, clouties are the most common well offering and will be found at most holy wells in bewildering abundance, even where no such tradition had previously existed.

The use of a cloutie forms a practice of popular healing magic, with correct procedure to be observed for efficacy. A piece of cloth, which may be as little as a single thread, must be pulled or torn, not cut, from the clothing worn by the patient, all the better if it is torn from that part of the clothing worn next to the ailing part. Alternatively, a piece of cloth may be tied about the ailing limb, and worn for a while before its removal at the well. This 'cloutie' is then dipped into the waters of the well before being hung upon an overhanging branch, or impaled upon a thorn. In some cases the cloutie might be secreted in a crevice between the stones surrounding a well. As the cloutie rots, so shall the ailment fade.

Sometimes a charm or prayer will be spoken, such as that used at a cloutie well on the Isle of Man: "I lift the water for the good of such and such a certain man, in the name of God, the Son and the Holy Ghost."[65] At other wells however, such as at Madron in Cornwall, complete silence was to be strictly observed throughout the rite.

---

64. Bord, Janet and Colin. *Cures and Curses – Ritual and Cult at Holy Wells*, p. 61.
65. Bord, Janet and Colin. *Cures and Curses – Ritual and Cult at Holy Wells*, p. 101.

Researcher of folk-magic and charming, Rose Mullins, tells us that a charm bag might sometimes be employed in place of the simple cloutie, with the aid of a magically inclined well-guardian. The bag would contain certain plant, animal and mineral matter, with something personal to the patient containing their vital essence, such as a lock of hair or nail parings. A cloutie; a piece of cloth worn next to the ailment, might also be included. It is explained that, by constructing such a charm, the spirit of the person would remain there, under the healing influence of the well.[66]

Clouties, like pins, were used to charm warts. The procedure at Ffynnon Cefn Lleithfan, Bryncroes, Gwynedd, involved a greased cloutie being hidden beneath a stone at the well's entrance.[67]

Superstition warns against the removal of clouties from a well, for it is believed that if anyone should do so, the ailment represented by the rag will be transferred unto them, in the same way that might occur if someone were to pick up discarded 'wart stones' or a 'get-lost-box' discarded in acts of 'passing-on' magic.[68] The touching of pins found in wart wells would likewise be avoided for fear of 'picking up' the warts they had been used to charm.

Just as is performed about the cauldron within the compass or 'castle' of the Art Magical; a ritual act, common to popular magical practice at many holy wells, particularly in Ireland to this day, is circumambulation. This is most often, but not in all cases, performed about the well in a 'sun-wise', deosil direction – the 'journey to the right'. It may of course be an invocation of the generative virtue and potency

---

66. Mullins, Rose. *White Witches – A Study of Charmers*, p. 8.
67. Bord, Janet and Colin. *Cures and Curses – Ritual and Cult at Holy Wells*, p. 21.
68. *Ibid.*

of the sun. The fact that complete circumambulations tend to be performed nine times, three times, or multiples thereof, suggest also a consideration for the tides and influences of the moon (associated in popular magic with change, transformation, death and rebirth), which, alongside the solar virtue may be thought naturally beneficial to acts of healing.

At some Cornish wells, the journey to the left, against the sun was employed within healing rites, possibly with the intent of banishing, or bringing about the 'death' of the ailment. In all cases circumambulation may appear to be an invocation of the diurnal motion of the heavenly virtues about the chthonic waters – as above, so below – bringing to mind again the generative potency of the creative act.

For many however, the 'journey to the left' was to be avoided for it would invite ill fortune. In The Highlands of Scotland we are told that the sun-wise direction is 'the lucky way', and all ritual movement about holy wells was made in this manner. Even the approach to a holy well was to be made from east to west on its south side.[69]

Circumambulation can form a central part of lengthy rites, involving various 'stations' at a well complex. A well in Tullybelton, Perthshire, was visited in the 1st of May, where the water of increased virtue would be imbibed, followed by the well and nearby standing stones each being circumambulated nine times.[70]

In Ireland a lengthy healing rite, involving circumambulation, was perfomed at least into the 20th century at a well complex at Dungiven, Londonderry. The well would be bowed to before being circumambulated in prayer. The patient would then bathe their hands and feet in the well before tearing a cloutie from their clothing to be hung upon an overhanging bush. From there they

---

69. Courtney, R.A. *Cornwall's Holy Wells – Their Pagan Origins*, p. 37.
70. Bord, Janet and Colin. Sacred Waters, p. 26.

would proceed to a large stone in the river Roe, there to bathe before circumambulating the stone, again in prayer. Further ceremonials would then be performed in the ruins of the church above the river, completed by more circumambulation around the ten foot tall Cloch-Patrick standing stone nearby.[71]

A less complex rite involving circumambulation and clouties was performed by those seeking a cure at the evocatively named Chibbyr Undin on the Isle of Man. Here, the patient would circumambulate the well twice, in the direction of the sun, whilst holding in their mouth water drawn from the well. A cloutie was then torn from their clothing, wetted with the well water in their mouth, before being hung upon the well's hawthorn.[72]

The circumambulation of wells remains an important part of the pilgrimage tradition in Ireland as a devotional practice of prayer, contemplation and meditation.

Once popularly observed as an essential step in the healing rites of many holy wells was the process of 'dream incubation'. This was the time when the patient, following the completion of healing rites at the well, would be left to sleep, often overnight, during which the healing influence was supposed to take effect. Incubation might take place upon a special mound beside the well (as at Madron in Cornwall) known as the saint's 'bed' and believed to be the burial place of the saint associated with the well. Incubation might also take place in a nearby church, house or inn.

In accordance with the power of time and tide, the waters of many wells were believed to be at their zenith of potency upon certain days of the year. As we have seen, in our exploration of creative act symbolism, early May was the perceived time of increased potency at many wells. It will be seen that Thursdays in early May were of

---

71. Ibid, p. 29-30.
72. Bord, Janet. *Cures and Curses – Ritual and Cult at Holy Wells*, p. 110.

importance in a number of cases, as was Ascension Day; which always falls upon a Thursday and usually in early May. The water of some holy wells in North Devonshire were believed to be at their most potent on Ascension Day morning, when water from such wells would be collected, bottled and taken home so that its curative virtue might be enjoyed throughout the year.[73]

Water was also bottled at holy wells in Ireland after midnight on the 1st of May. This water, named 'The Purity of the Well' was believed to be most potent against the malefic powers of witchcraft, and was kept throughout the year as a protective household charm against ill-wishing and the evil eye.[74]

A similar tradition existed at many wells where the first water to be drawn on New Year's Day was named 'The Flower of the Well'. At some wells, the first visitor on New Year's Day would leave a sign that 'The Flower' of that well had been taken, such as by dropping a flower onto the surface of the water. This potent water was bottled and kept as a household charm for good fortune. The Flower of the Well from three specific wells in Wark on Tyne, Northumberland, had the additional ability to impart upon the first to imbibe of it extraordinary magical powers, such as the power to fly through the air by night, or to pass through a key-hole.[75] These three wells were the Old Kirk Well, the Upper Well and the Riverside Well.

Summer's zenith – Midsummer and St John the Baptist's Day, was unsurprisingly also a time when the waters of some wells were believed to be at their most potent. At midnight on St John's Eve, the 23rd of June, it was believed in Ireland that the water of wells dedicated to St John

---

73. Whitlock, Ralph. *The Folklore of Devon*, p. 147.
74. Bord, Janet and Colin. Sacred Waters, p. 109.
75. Bord, Janet. Cures and Curses – Ritual and Cult at Holy Wells, p. 49.

the Baptist would boil, and, for the first hour of St John's Day, these wells had the power to cure any illness.[76]

The festival of Lammas, the 1st of August, was believed to be the time of maximum potency for wells on the Isle of Man which would be popularly visited upon this day. The old Manx, however, retained their old name for this festival; 'Lal Lhuanys' well into the 19th century. It has been suggested that this name is likley to indicate the old Manx observance of this festival was connected with the Celtic god Lugh.[77]

When carrying home the potent waters, it was important to observe certain taboos. Keeping silence during the carrying of well water was important, just as it was to observe total silence during rites at some wells.

It was also vital that the container holding the water did not touch the ground, and was not to be put down until the water's destination was reached; such as the bedside of a patient to benefit from the water's curative influence.[78] This observance is rather reminiscent of the folk-magical taboo that charms, such as the virgin nail, should not be allowed to touch the ground whereupon their power would be lost.

Taboos, allied to silence, to be observed within cloutie magic at some wells might include performing the rite in secret; telling no one of the visit to the well. After the rite had been completed, the rout taken home should be different to that taken to the well.[79]

Other taboos which could result in the powers of the well itself being withdrawn by the offended well spirit, sometimes along with dire consequences for the perpetrator, include women washing clothes in the well, the felling of well-side trees and bathing animals in a holy well,

---

76. Bord, Janet and Colin. *Sacred Waters*, p. 57.
77. Ibid, p. 34.
78. Bord, Janet. *Cures and Curses – Ritual and Cult at Holy Wells*, p. 65.
79. Whelan, Edna. *The Magic and Mystery of Holy Wells*, p. 64.

or allowing animals to drink from them where their use is supposed to be reserved for humans only.[80]

In Cornwall, the spirit of the well of St. Phillack was so offended when, in 1720, Erasmus Pascoe, the Sheriff of Cornwall bathed his dog in its waters that a dreadful curse fell upon him and his family.[81]

Some wells, however, were believed to be particularly possessed of the virtue to cure animals. In Wales there were wells said to have the power to cure animals such as cattle, dogs, horses, sheep and pigs.[82]

Where the illness or injury of cattle was believed to be the result of malefic witchcraft, or the evil eye, water would be drawn from a well and 'silvered' by being poured over a new silver coin. This charm-water was given to the cattle to lift the ill-influence and to act as a protection against further supernatural interference.[83]

The spirits of some wells appear to have been happy to provide cures for both humans and animals. In Harpham, St John's Well was visited by humans seeking cures for sore eyes and headaches, whilst farmers would consult the powers of the well to tame wild bulls.[84]

The world famous Roman baths and hot springs of the city of Bath were said to have been first established as a healing centre, and dedicated to the Celtic Goddess Sulis following the healing of a Celtic prince and his pigs. Prince Bladud, badly afflicted with leprosy, was outcast from court and took on the work of swine-herding. He took his pigs, also afflicted with skin infections and sores, to drink from the spring and observed, after their wallowing in the spring's mud, that

---

80. Bord, Janet and Colin. *Sacred Waters*, p. 100-101.
81. Straffon, Cheryl. *Fentynyow Kernow*, p. 47.
82. Bord, Janet. *Cures and Curses – Ritual and Cult at Holy Wells*, p. 69.
83. Bord, Janet and Colin. *Sacred Waters*, p. 110.
84. Whelan, Edna. *The Magic and Mystery of Holy Wells*, p. 57.

their condition soon cleared. Bladud decided to try the spring's virtues for himself and bathed in its waters and was healed of his affliction.[85]

～ Healing ～

The seeking of curative virtues would seem to have been the most common intent behind the practice of folk-magic at holy wells. Just as Cornish tradition tells us that long queues of clients would form at the door of the 19th century white witch, charmer or peller in the Spring; the time at which their powers were believed to be renewed, so too would pilgrims queue in large numbers, at the times of potency, to benefit from the powers of the well and its guardian spirit.[86]

It would be both superfluous and beyond the scope of this brief work to here list the many healing wells of the British Isles, and the ailments they would cure; a number of excellent books have achieved this task. Here shall be described but some of the notable healing wells with associated rites and ceremonies of curative operative magic.

Beginning close to home, Madron Well is perhaps the most famous and visited of Cornwall's curative holy wells. Madron is a 'cloutie well' as will become all to apparent to anyone who makes the long walk down the narrow muddy path, lined with tangled branches thickly adorned with lichens. Beside the path, near its end, trees overhanging an area of shallow water are completely festooned with all manner of 'clouties', of which sadly only a small number, if any, will be the 'genuine article'. For the genuine cloutie spell to have any efficacy, the cloutie itself must be of natural, biodegradable material; as it rots, so shall the illness it represents fade. A quick glance at the technicolour display of sometimes bizarre objects and materials, bound tightly about the tree

---

85. Ibid, p. 16.
86. Ibid, p. 62.

branches, reveals that the synthetic is now firmly the order of the day. The original ritual and purpose of the cloutie is clearly unknown to the majority of Madron's visitors today, and the modern practice appears to be a general 'offering', perhaps accompanied by the making of a wish.

This, however, is not the location of the well proper, which is hidden deeper in the tangled and extremely boggy wood. Clouties found here are far fewer in number, and are more likely to resemble the genuine article, indicating perhaps that the old rite is still carried out by those 'in the know'.

Whilst 'clouties' may be found habitually tied to the branches of trees growing in the vicinity of most holy wells in Cornwall today, it was noted in the mid 19th century that the practice appeared to be confined to Madron only, and was entirely unobserved at other Cornish wells.[87]

---

87. Quiller-Couch, Thomas. *Ancient and Holy Wells of Cornwall*, p. 132.

Nearby is the beautiful well chapel, with its font in the south-west corner, fed continuously by a musical flow of water from the same source as the well proper. This font is itself considered a holy well, and also has its healing traditions.

Madron was generally considered powerful in the curing of all manner of afflictions and injuries, but was particularly noted for the curing of skin diseases and rickets.[88] The measurable properties of the water in the well chapel have shown it to have extremely high radiation levels; over double the background levels for the environment, and 49% higher than levels found in the chapel interior. Calcium levels were found to be at a concentration of 20.20mg/litre, which may account for the well's reputation for curing rickets and other bone related afflictions.[89]

A 19th century guardian of the well, an elderly woman known as An Kitty, appears to have been the keeper of the well's rites and traditions, and would give its visitors instruction in the correct procedures which were to be conducted in strict silence.

The rite for curing children involved the child first being striped naked before being immersed in the waters of the well three times against the sun. The child was then passed three or nine times with the sun around the well before being wrapped and placed to sleep for a while on St Maddern's Bed, which was a grassy mound beside the well.[90] If the child slept, and the water of the well bubbled, it was taken as a sign that the cure would be granted.[91] The rite would be concluded by a strip of clothing being torn from the child's chothing and hung from an overhanging thorn branch by the well.

---

88. Johnson, Nicholas. Rose, Peter. *Cornwall's Archaeological Heritage*, p. 33.
89. Straffon, Cheryl. *Ancient Sites in West Penwith*, p. 40.
90. Straffon, Cheryl. Pagan Cornwall – *Land of the Goddess*, p. 46.
91. Courtney, R.A. *Cornwall's Holy Wells – Their Pagan Origins*, p. 36.

The Magic of Springs & Holy Wells

Adults to be cured would also be stripped naked before circumambulating about the well thrice against the sun, and then thrice with the sun. A cloutie, torn from the patient's clothing would then be left with the wise-woman guardian to be hung from a 'faery thorn'.[92] The remarkable healing virtues of the well had been confirmed in 1640, by the restoring to health of John Trelille who, for sixteen years had not had the use of his legs following a cruel injury inflicted upon his spine. In a dream, he was told that the use of his legs would be restored unto him, if he bathed in the waters of 'St. Maderne'. Upon the first three Thursdays in May, he visited, bathed in the waters and slept upon 'St. Maderne's Bed', which in this case we are told was a grassy mound located next to the stone altar in the well chapel, built anew each year by local people. As a result of these rites, the use of his legs was restored, and he was quite cured enough to gain employment before enlisting in the king's army, only to be slain in 1644.

In the late 18th century, two men, John Thomas and William Cork, both without the use of their legs, resorted to 'St. Mardren's Well' on Corpus Christi evening – Holy Thursday, to make some small offering there, to drink of the well and lie beside it upon the earth through the night. In the morning, they drank once more, before each bottling some of the well's water to take away with them. Upon seeing improvement in their condition within three weeks, both men decided to follow the procedure again on the same night the following year. As a result, both were able to go about with the aid of a stick, John Thomas was eventually able to work well as a fisherman, and William Cork became a soldier, losing his life in service.

It is likely that the mysterious 'Saint Madron', who is usually referred to as a 'he' may be a derivation of the Welsh female St Madern. Certainly the saint has a

---

92. Howard, Michael. *West Country Witches*, p. 27.

presence in Cornwall, with two churches dedicated to her: Minster Church, Boscastle, and Tintagel Parish Church. It is also suggested that Madron, and indeed St Madrun, may derive from Modron; the Welsh 'Divine Mother' goddess. Her presence in Cornwall is revealed via her son, Mabon, giving his name unto St Mabyn.[93]

It is interesting to note that, in the late 19th century, the elderly guardian of the well stated that she had never heard of any saint having anything to do with the well, and believed the association to have been imposed upon the place by visiting Victorian gentry.[94]

The wells of Chapel Euny, straddling an ancient track-way and close to the ancient courtyard settlement of Carn Euny with its mysterious fogou, were also an important locus for the curative rites of popular well-magic. The better preserved of the two, known as 'The Giant's Well', had a strong reputation for general curative virtue, but particularly effective for wounds and sores. Like some other Cornish wells, it was believed to protect those baptised using its waters from hanging by a hempen rope; a power that has proven to be untrue of this well.[95]

Dr. Borlase, visiting the well in the mid-18th century, observed two women performing a healing rite for a young child, and, around a century later, antiquarian Richard Edmonds observed the same rite still in use at the well.[96]

The traditional procedure was to visit the well upon the first three Wednesdays in May, one hour before noon, where the ailing child would be dipped thrice in the waters against the sun, and then dragged upon the ground around the well, thrice and in the same direction.

---

93. Straffon, Cheryl. *Pagan Cornwall – Land of the Goddess*, p. 67.
94. Cooke, Ian. *Mermaid to Merrymaid – Journey to the Stones*, p. 105.
95. Ibid, p. 106.
96. Ibid.

The Magic of Springs & Holy Wells

Also once popularly visited upon the first three Wednesdays in May, is the beautiful and secluded little well of Alsia, not far from St Buryan. Like Madron it had a particularly strong reputation for curing rickets in children alongside other ailments and weakness. Fights were known to break out during the time of pilgrimage between the mothers performing rites there, and local women who objected to babies being dipped in their supply of drinking water![97]

Healing rites were also performed for weak and sickly children deep within a most chthonic and mysterious setting. A cave in Cornwall's Holywell Bay, Cubert, is home to a well; its waters gently cascading down through multileveled smooth rock basins, streaked with pale green, pink and red mineral deposits. To venture within this strange cavern of colour is like entering a portal to the Otherworld, and here, mothers would bring their children seeking the curative virtues of the magical waters. Here, the child would be dipped within the waters and passed through an aperture connecting two of the rock basins. The most potent times for these rites were Ascension Day and the 1st of November[98] – a most fitting date for a journey into such an Otherworldly location.

It is perhaps the liminality of water that leads to a sense of the Otherworldly and the numinous in the presence of streams, pools and wells. As a window to the Underworld, or a mirror to the heavens, deep associations with vision and the divine are inherent within the old beliefs surrounding water. Herein, we find old traditions linking water with the 'Eye of God', and superstitions, cognate with those that warn against seeing one's reflection captured within a pool, that warn against staring into flowing waters, for to

---
97. Quiller-Couch, Thomas. *Ancient and Holy Wells of Cornwall*, p. 4-5.
98. Straffon, Cheryl. *Fentynyow Kernow*, p. 54.

do so is to stare into God's own eye. Intimations of such beliefs may be exemplified in the many 'eye-wells' where the chthonic waters are believed to be possessed of the powers to heal sore eyes and restore clarity of vision.

In Cornwall, such wells have included Blisland Holy Well, a well at Castle Horneck near Penzance, Joan's Pitcher Well in Lewannick, Collurian Well near Ludgvan, St James's Well in St. Breward and Roche Holy Well. The name of Collurion Well may come from 'kollurion'; a Greek word meaning 'eye-salve'.[99]

At Roche Holy Well, at and St James's Well, the rite of bathing afflicted eyes involved calling for the favour of the tutelary saint before offering a bent pin unto the waters. The same offering was made to the eye-well of Whitford, Flintshire.[100]

A slightly more elaborate rite, which may have been for the healing of a child's eyes, was observed at St Anthony's Well, Edinburgh in the 19th century. Three women were assembled around the well; two of them elderly, who together appeared to oversee and conduct the rite, and the young woman holding a small child. The elderly women produced cups from their pockets, and filled them from the well to drink of its waters. A cup was likewise filled for the younger woman to drink, and again for the child. Next a long bandage cloth was immersed fully in the well by one of the elderly women, before being withdrawn, wrung out and immersed for a second time. It was then withdrawn again and bound about the child's head so that the eyes were covered. Before departing, a bottle was filled from the well, probably for further curative use, or to be kept as a charm.[101]

---

99. Ibid, p. 40.
100. Henderson, William. *Witchcraft, Toadlore and Charms of the Northern Counties*, p. 53.
101. Bord, Janet and Colin. *Sacred Waters*, p. 50.

Whilst many curative well rites were fairly simple and brief in nature, longer and more involved rites, often employing overnight incubation, appear to have been requisite for the condition of epilepsy.

At the Welsh well of St Thecla, or Ffynnon Tegla, Denbighshire, the patient was taken to the well to be bathed in its waters, whilst offerings of coins were made. The patient then had to circumambulate the well four times whilst repeating the Lord's Prayer. Another rite at the well called for the involvement of a black cockerel or a hen. The sex of the bird corresponded to that of the patient and the rite had to be conducted upon a Friday, after sunset. It was begun by the cockerel or hen being carried three times around the churchyard, after which the rite was relocated to the well where the unfortunate bird was pricked with a pin and thrown in. The rite was then relocated again to the church, where the all night incubation would begin. With the Bible for a pillow, and the altar-cloth for a blanket, the patient would be placed to sleep beneath the communion table. The patient breathed into the beak of the bird, thus presumably transferring the affliction, and if it were dead by the morning, the rite would be successful.[102]

The rite of incubation was employed by those seeking a cure for epilepsy from the well of St Beuno, where the patient would bathe in the well before sleeping overnight upon a bed of rushes prepared on the tombstone of the saint.[103]

Historically, the treatment of the mentally ill has rarely been a delicate affair, and the same is true with well-cures where the rites conducted for the treatment of madness were sometimes of a decidedly brutal nature.

Bowssening was a ritual procedure employed at some Cornish wells in pursuit of a cure for the insane. At St

---

102. Howard, Michael. *Welsh Witches and Wizards*, p. 138-139.
103. Bord, Janet and Colin. *Sacred Waters*, p. 214.

Non's Well, Altarnun, the patient was set to stand with their back to the well pool, and sent flying headfirst into the water via a strong and sudden blow to their chest. Within the pool, a strong man took hold of the patient and violently and repeatedly pushed them under the water again and again. The exhausted patient was then taken into the church where masses would be said over them. The same procedure was followed at St Cleer's Well.[104]

A far gentler procedure however was followed on the Isle of Man at St Ronan's Well. The patient was circumambulated around the ruins of the Temple of St Molochus. A hereditary guardian would then bring water, drawn from the well in a special vessel in their keeping, which was then sprinkled upon the patient. The rite was concluded with a period of incubation upon the place where the altar once stood and the success of the rite was signalled by the patient sleeping soundly.[105]

Another gentle, if rather uncomfortable, procedure was used at St Fillan's Well, Perthshire. The patient would be immersed within the well before being taken to the nearby chapel for an overnight incubation, where they were left, bound, and with the chapel's bell placed over their head.[106]

Divination

Given the old beliefs surrounding wells and sacred springs as a ritual locus of pilgrimage, where one may initiate exchange with the Otherworldly and seek Divine wisdom and vision via the agency of

---

104. Johnson, Nicholas. Rose, Peter. *Cornwall's Archaeological Heritage*, p. 23.
105. Bord, Janet and Colin. *Sacred Waters*, p. 59.
106. Howard, Michael. *Scottish Witches & Warlocks*, p. 15.

indwelling spirits, or of the human well guardian as a spiritual intermediary, it is of no surprise the holy wells should possess a rich tradition of divinatory and prophetic use.

Some of the divinatory purposes for which the people would resort to holy wells were much the same as those commonly sought from professional witches, wise-women and cunning men; such as for matters of love and matrimony, or to discover the identity of thieves and the whereabouts of lost property. For such services a sometimes hefty fee would be required by the professional folk-magical practitioner, thus the holy well could have represented a more economical recourse for such matters.

At a number of prophetic wells however, the presence of a guardian wise-woman would be required, for, it was believed, the rites would require her advice or assistance for efficacy, or perhaps, only she could mediate or interpret for the spirits of the well.

One such Cornish well, now no longer extant, was the prophetic holy well of Gulval. Here, in the first half of the 18th century, the well was cared for by an elderly woman who appears to have acted as its 'high priestess'; instructing visitors in the virtues and rites of the potent waters. Gulval Well was widely reputed for its powers to reveal the location of lost cattle, or that of stolen property. Also, it was possessed of the ability to reveal unto the enquirer whether absent friends were living or deceased. If living, the friend's state of health could also be gleaned from the spirit of the waters. The name of the friend had only to be spoken over the waters, and, if dead, they would remain still and quiet. If they were living but in ill health, the waters would begin to bubble and cloud with mud. If however they lived in good health, bubbles would arise to the surface; the waters remaining of crystalline clarity.

Wisht Waters

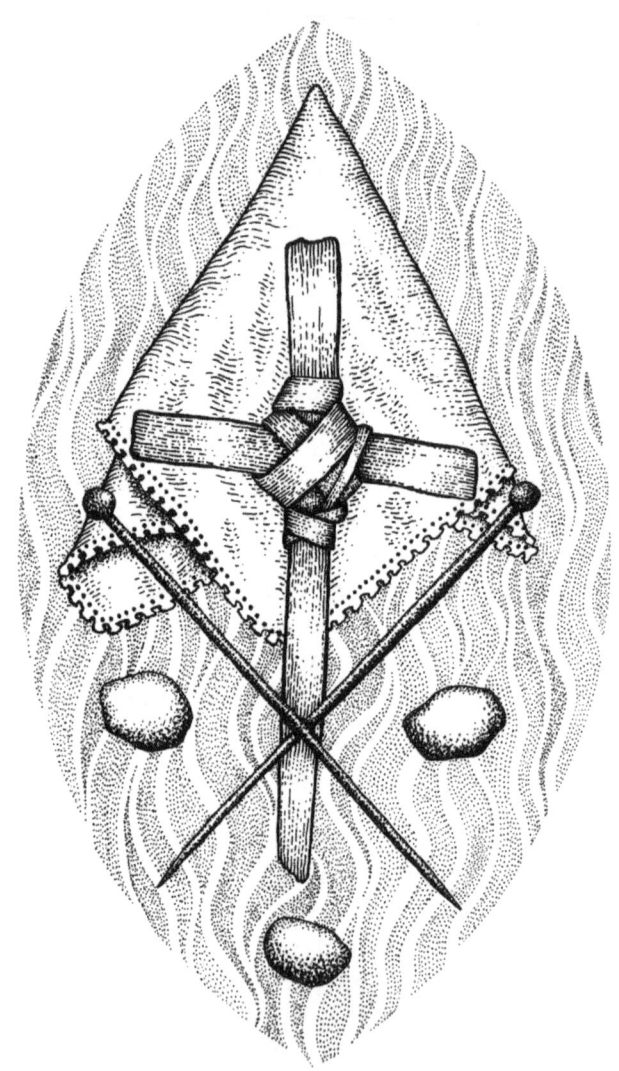

As with curative well magic, the offerings made during popular rites of divination at holy wells included such things as pins and pebbles. Often it was the offering unto the waters that activated the prophetic powers, via bubbles rising to the surface, or the waters acting upon the offering, causing it to move in a certain manner.

It was both bubbles and the movement of offerings that would be read in divinations for matters of love at Alsia Well. On the first three Wednesdays in May, many young women would gather at the well, there to learn the fate of named young couples. Two pins, or pebbles, would be dropped into the water, and their actions as they sank to the bottom closely observed. If the two settled together, then the couple were to join together in matrimony. If, however, they settled apart from one another, then the couple were destined to part company. The number of bubbles sent to the surface would foretell the number of years until the prophesised union or separation. Love divinations would also be made at Alsia by floating bramble leaves on the water's surface. Such were also popularly used in conjunction with spring water in the folk-magical charming of burns.

At other Cornish wells, such as at St Euny's Well, Menacuddle Well and at Roche Holy Well (on Holy Thursday), readings would also be made of the number of bubbles sent up by the offering of pins or pebbles. Coins were used as well as pins in divinations at Jesus Well, St. Minver.

The offering of pins however might also produce prophetic visions within a well's waters. At St Caradog's Well, Haverfordwest, Pembrokeshire, an offering of three pins was required of any woman who sought, on Easter Monday, to conjure forth a vision of the face of her future husband.[107]

Other prophetic wells required crosses of straw, rushes, or a Palm Sunday cross, the movements of which would provide the signs to be read.

At Holy Well, Bodmin, young people would fashion crosses by tying rushes gathered from the nearby marsh. These they would set to float upon the water with a spoken charm which, like the well itself, is now sadly lost.

---

107. Bord, Janet and Colin. *Sacred Waters*, p. 88.

The brave could discover whether or not they would outlive the year by visiting the holy well of Our Lady of Nance, Colan, on Palm Sunday. There, an offering of money and a palm cross was required; the cross was put into the well, the money into the hand of the priest![108] If the cross did float upon the water, the enquirer would live to see the following year, if it sank however, death was predicted to be near.

For love divinations, a cross was required at Madron Well, fashioned from two inch long pieces of straw, affixed at their midst with a pin. This was to be floated on the well's water on May Morning, the first Sunday in May, or the first three Thursdays in May, whereupon the spirit of the well would send bubbles rising from its depths. The number of bubbles produced foretold the number of years until matrimony. Alternatively, two pins or pebbles might be employed to consult the spirit of the well in the very same manner as employed at Alsia. The use of straw crosses and pins put into Madron Well for wishes is remembered by elderly locals as still taking place in the 1930s.[109]

Clothing and personal items such as handkerchiefs might be used, via which it would appear the spirit of the well was able to 'read' the fortune of the enquirer. Rites of love divination were conducted on Anglesey by the old wise-woman guardian of Crochan Llanddwyn – 'The Crochan Cauldron' in the 19th century. On the 25th of January, the feast day of St Dwynwen, to whom the well was dedicated, young people would visit to make wishes or divine their prospects in love. After paying a fee to the old woman, she would take the client's handkerchief and lay it upon the surface of the well's waters in order to read their future by interpreting the movements of eels living in the spring. If bubbles

---

108. Straffon, Cheryl. *Fentynyow Kernow*, p. 54.
109. Straffon, Cheryl. *Ancient Sites in West Penwith*, p. 40.

appeared during the reading, it was a fortunate omen of happiness in matters of love.[110]

At another Anglesey well, Ffynnon Gybi, handkerchiefs were also used in love divinations, or a feather might be employed instead. If the item, laid upon the water's surface, began to move in a southward direction, the well had revealed that the enquirer's lover was honourable, but dishonourable if it instead moved towards the north.

At some wells, the sick would have their chances of recovery divined by the use of clothing. Such a method was employed at Ffynnon Gelynin – 'The Well of St. Celynin' in the Conwy valley, North Wales. At this little well beside the beautiful and remote Llangelynin Church, ailing children would be bathed, wrapped and taken to a farmhouse nearby for an overnight period of incubation. An article of the child's clothing would be placed into the well where a good omen of recovery was given if the clothing floated. If it sank however, death was prophesised.[111]

When water was drawn from the Head Well, Whitchurch, Buckinghamshire, to be brought to the bedside of a patient, their chances of recovery would also be divined via their clothing. The article would be placed upon the water; its floating foretold recovery, and death by its sinking.[112]

On the Isle of Lewis, the waters of St Andrew's Well possessed the power read a patient's chances of recovery from a wooden bowl used to draw water for them. After the water had been brought to the patient's bedside, the bowl would be returned to the well and floated upon its surface. Here, if the bowl turned in a sun-wise direction, recovery could be expected, but death was indicated should the bowl turn against the sun.

---

110. Howard, Michael. *Welsh Witches and Wizards*, p. 139-140.
111. Bord, Janet and Colin. *Sacred Waters*, p. 216.
112. Bord, Janet. *Cures and Curses – Ritual and Cult at Holy Wells*, p. 69.

The movement of two straws were used for the same purpose at the Black Isle well of Craigie, Avoch. Here, on the first Sunday in May, the straws were floated upon the water, if they began to turn in opposite directions a recovery was indicated, but death if they remained still.[113]

Offerings of food might also coax the water spirits into making revelations. Chink Well, Portrane, Dublin, was washed by the high tides of the sea, and here bread would be left at the wells edge. If it was taken by the tide, a cure was assured.[114]

By such food offerings could the identity of thieves be revealed by the well spirits. At Ffynnon Bedrog, Gwynedd, the one injured by theft could drop a piece of bread into the well and begin to speak the names of all those suspected of the offence. Upon speaking the name of the thief, the piece of bread would sink beneath the waters. This was also a well of healing, and pins would have been employed within its rites, for a vessel of dark stone was long ago brought up from its bottom and found to be full of pins.[115]

The old rites were not all necessarily performed at the well itself, for the water may be drawn forth and taken home for the practice of divinations. This would seem to suggest that, as with water drawn from a well and brought into the home for curative and protective purposes, the prophetic spirit and virtue remains present within the very water when brought away from its locus of springing forth.

The popular old love divination involving written names rolled into balls of clay, sometimes called specifically for water drawn from a spring to enhance

---

113. Bord, Janet and Colin. *Sacred Waters*, p. 237.

114. Bord, Janet and Colin. *Sacred Waters*, p. 59.

115. Baring-Gould, Sabine and Fisher, John. *The Lives of the British Saints Volume 4*, p. 102.

the rite's efficacy. This was particularly the case when the Romany employed the method.[116] The enquirer would write the name of each of her suitors upon slips of paper; rolling each of these separately into a ball of clay. Upon one slip however, she would write her own name. the balls of clay were dropped into the vessel of water and anxiously watched as the clay dissolved to gradually free the slips of paper. The first name to rise to the surface was the suitor the enquirer was prophesised to marry. If, however, it was her own name that arose first to the surface then she will remain unwed.[117]

The spirit of the well was not always dependant upon the presence of humans or their rituals in order to issue prophecy and omen. 'Drumming Wells' are so named for the strange, sometimes loud, and as yet unexplained drumming sounds that they occasionally produced. The occurrence of the drumming sound was often taken to be ominous of significant national events, or of the fate of royalty and noble families, particularly in foretelling deaths. Perhaps such links associated the spirit of such wells with the sovereignty and sanctity of the land?

Belief in the oracular powers of the sacred spring and holy well is truly ancient. Around a well sacred to the goddess Demeter, the ancient Greeks would perform complex rites in order to receive oracular vision regarding life and death. Offerings of prayer and sacrifice would be made, and a mirror suspended over the well by cords, wherein the enquirer would be shown visions that would reveal unto them the fate of their longevity.[118]

---

116. Buckland, Raymond. *Gypsy Witchcraft and Magic*, p. 50.
117. Gurdon, Eveline Camilla (Ed.). *Old Suffolk Love and Cure Charms*, p. 25-26.
118. Whelan, Edna. *The Magic and Mystery of Holy Wells*, p. 77.

The Wishing Well

Whilst rites of healing and divination appear to have been the most widely employed forms of popular well magic, the act of wishing has today surpassed all other magical uses for wells. The magical wishing well has become archetypal, and is perhaps the reason why so many wells, real or artificial, and ornamental fountains and pools attract habitual and instinctual offerings of coin. Wishing; essentially a simple and general form of spell casting, is however an old and traditional aspect of well magic, with a varied set of rituals.

As with other matters of well magic, the offering of pins was required by the spirits of some wells in order for the spell of wishing to have efficacy.

That the agency of spirits was believed to be central to such procedures is confirmed in the wishing wells named after the faery folk. The beautiful little Fairy Well, situated high within a cliff overlooking Cornwall's Carbis Bay is regarded still as a potent wishing well. Here the wish must be spoken aloud to the spirits and accompanied by the offering of a crooked pin. Another Cornish wishing well in a rather extraordinary setting is the Giant's Well on St Michael's Mount where pins were offered as wishes were made.

Not far from St Austell the spirits of Menacuddle Well, inhabiting an enchanting moss-covered well house, would grant wishing in exchange for a crooked pin. Here, the well pilgrim might see the well's previously offered pins arise to greet the newly offered pin on its descent.

The practice was not of course isolated to Cornwall and appears to have been particularly common at wells throughout the North of England. At the North Yorkshire well of St John, Mount Grace Priory, those seeking to make a wish must float a pin upon the water by sticking it first through an ivy leaf.[119]

---

119. Whelan, Edna. *The Magic and Mystery of Holy Wells*, p. 76.

Sancreed Well, Sancreed Cornwall

Oscar and the author visit St Anne's Well, Whitstone, North Cornwall.

Facing: the enigmatic carved stone head within St Anne's well-house.

St Germoe's early Norman font carved with three strikingly primitive heads.

St Tielo's Skull-Cup, Llandaff Cathedral – Eglwys Gadeiriol Llandaf.

Oscar and the author visit St Neot's Well, St Neot, Cornwall.

Below: the legend of the three fish of the well.

Facing: peering through the well-house door into the interior.

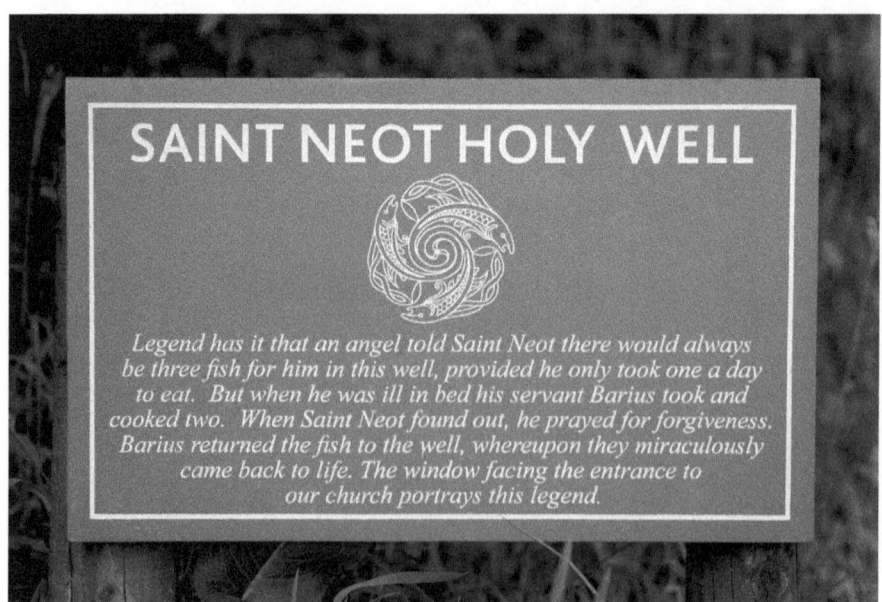

The creative conjunction of solar and lunar influences: at the foot of Roche Rock, dedicated to Saint Michael, is said to exist a well, ebbing and flowing with the tide.

Below: Jesus Well at St Minver, where the sacred waters sprang forth when an unidentified traveling saint grew thirsty and thrust his staff into the parched sand dunes.

Alsia Well, West Cornwall.

Left: St Nun's Well, known as the Piskies' Well, near Pelynt, Cornwall.

Above: the granite basin inside the well, said to have returned here by supernatural agency after having been removed by a farmer.

Fice's Well, Dartmoor and its circular enclosure.

Other offerings to please were made during acts of wishing, however, at St Faith's Well, Hertford in the 17th century, such rites were overseen by a priest who it was believed possessed the power, via the well, to either grant or deny wishes. If the priest was pleased with the offering, the object placed in the well would float and the wish would be granted. If dissatisfied however, he would cause the object to sink thus denying the petitioner that which they wish for.[1]

Pebbles would be offered in wishing rites at St Anne's Well, Trellech, Monmouthshire, which also had a divinatory element. Following the offering of a pebble, the spirit of the well would indicate the result via bubbles. Many bubbles indicated the wish had been granted, few bubbles meant that there would be a delay, but if no bubbles appeared, the petition had failed.[2]

Offerings however were not required at all wells. In the Quantock Hills, one might conduct a simple wishing rite by visiting a spring under the cover of night. There one should whisper that which is desired three times before making a 'criss-cross' sign above the water. In performing this rite, the wish is always granted, but, we are warned, not always in a way the petitioner would like.[3]

Drinking the water was a requisite feature of some wishing rites at wells. The rite to be performed at Upwey Well, Dorsetshire, requires drawing water with a glass, turning to stand with one's back to the well, drinking a little of the water from the glass before throwing the rest back into the well over one's shoulder.

On the isle of Barra, fishermen would wish for good herring catches by visiting St Clair's Well on Sundays to drink of its waters.[4]

---

1. Bord, Janet and Colin. *Sacred Waters*, p. 91.
2. Ibid, p. 220.
3. Bord, Janet. Cures and Curses – *Ritual and Cult at Holy Wells*, p. 36.
4. Bord, Janet and Colin. *Sacred Waters*, p. 108.

Curse Magic & Protections

Just as the witch was traditionally skilled in grey magic, and the dual ways of cures and curses, so too were some wells possessed of 'double ways' powers, to bless or to blast.

The enactment of rites of cursing at wells and springs in the British Isles can be traced back at least to the Roman period. The magic of ill-wishing, retaliation and binding draws upon and is associated with spirits and powers of a 'darker' nature. It is perhaps for this reason, and for the liminality of water; as a point of access to the Otherworldly, or the Underworld itself, that wells hold a central role in ancient traditions of curse magic. Such magic in the Roman era often employed lead; a suitably 'dark' and Saturnine material, lending useful virtues of binding and restriction unto such operations. Curse tablets, defixiones, were formed from sheets of lead, inscribed with the ill intent of the curse, and the name of the victim. The tablet would often be rolled, or folded, before being stuck through with a nail; a magical act of defigo; 'pinning down' or 'fixing' one's will and intent upon the target of one's work. Such an act is not isolated to malefic working, and is cognate with the 'creative act' and fertility; giving life unto the magician's will. In curse magic however the act embodies the triune powers of torment, fixing and intent-enlivenment.

The completed defixio was then, in further conjuration of the Underworld virtues and dark intent upon the victim, buried in the ground, or dropped into the chthonic waters of a well.

Around forty such lead tablets have been discovered in Bath; home of the sacred springs of Sulis-Minerva.[5] The use of nail-impaled lead defixiones survived long into

---
5. Bord, Janet and Colin. *Sacred Waters*, p. 86.

modern period folk-magical tradition; continued within the British Isles to very recent times. In the Museum of Witchcraft in Cornwall's Boscastle are three lead defixiones; each a roll of sheet lead, two of which have been struck through with an iron nail. These examples were found in Blisland, Madron, and St Germans.

A well which became heavily associated with popular curse magic from the late 18th century, and around which complex rites of ill-wishing had grown, was Ffynnon Eilian on Anglesey. Some of these rites employed curse tablets which were made from slate, being more readily available than sheet lead, and easy to inscribe.

The desire for magical retaliation against one's enemies was such that it provided lucrative business for the well's guardians who, for a fee, oversaw and assisted in the rites of cursing. In order to place a curse via a tablet at the well, the well guardian would enter the victim's name in a book, and supply the client with a slate onto which the enemy's initials would be inscribed before being dropped into the well whilst the curse was uttered.

A remarkable example of such a curse tablet was discovered in the well in 1925. The small slate is inscribed with the letters 'RF' which are large and taken to be initials, along with faint smaller letters in the four corners. These appear to be possibly 'OAM', 'MEM', 'AGM' and 'M'. The whole is framed with a 'net' of crossed lines. In the centre of the slate, between the large initials, is a waxen image; the figure has been stuck through its midst with a pin, and its left arm broken off.

Curse rites at the well employing image magic involved the wax effigies being stuck with pins whilst secret curses were uttered. The image would then be immersed in the well three times before being dropped in the well and left.

Another rite, repeated thrice, involved a pin being dropped into the well as the enemy's name was spoken. The guardian of the well spoke from the bible as the curser drank some of the well water from a cup before throwing the remainder over their head as the curse was uttered. A most horrible rite performed at this well involved skewering a frog which was to be floated upon the well's water, the skewer's ends having been pushed into corks. As long as the unfortunate creature remained alive, the victim of the curse would suffer.

Pieces of paper were employed in place of tablets in cursing rites at Ffynnon Gybi, also on Anglesey. Upon these the victims' names would be written, before being hidden under the well's bank.[6] Presumably, as the paper began to disintegrate, so the victim would suffer. At another Anglesey cursing well, Ffynoon Estyn, people would seek to magically harm their enemies by throwing bent pins into the water.[7] The same process of ill-wishing was employed at Llanlawer Holy Well, Pembrokshire.[8]

Curse tablets, waxen images, papers and crooked pins were not always required within well rites of ill-wishing; at Devil's Whispering Well, Somerset, it was enough to simply whisper the curse to the well's waters.

Curses could also be lifted at wells, a belief which provided further income for the guardians of Anglesey's Ffynnon Eilian, who, for a much larger fee than they took for assisting the placing of the curse in the first place, provided a curse-lifting service for the well's victims. In the early 19th century, the well was providing an annual income of nearly £300.[9] Those who suspected they might be the victim of a curse rite at the well would enquire with the well's guardian, who could look to see if their name had been entered in the book of those who had been 'put in the well'. If this was so, complex rites

---

6. Bord, Janet and Colin. *Sacred Waters*, p. 84.
7. Howard, Michael. *Welsh Witches and Wizards*, p. 139.
8. Bord, Janet and Colin. *Sacred Waters*, p. 223.
9. Ibid, p. 84.

would be performed at the well, these involved Psalms being read from the Bible and circumambulations around the waters. The well would also be drained by the guardian so that the victim's curse slate could be found and removed, ground into a fine powder and mixed with salt. Then, a fire was built upon which the mixture was burnt. Further measures continued at the victim's home, for the well's water was bottled for them to take away. This had to be drunk with the reading of certain Psalms.

Testament to the absolute belief in the powers of the well is the story of one of its victims. In the latter part of the 19th century, a man was found not to have left the boundaries of his home in Montgomery in many years. He had gone to the guardian of Ffynnon Eilian and discovered that his name had been marked on a slate and put into the well. Paying the required fee, he underwent the rites of curse lifting, a condition of which was that he was never, under any circumstance, to leave the bounds of his property again. From young manhood to old age he faithfully followed this instruction.

Such was the fear of being cursed at Ffynnon Eilian that the threat was used amongst the locals; "mi 'th rof yn Ffynnon Elian!" which meant "I'll put thee in Elian's Well!".[10]

A major role of certain curative wells was the lifting of the effects of ill-wishing and black bewitchments. At Ffynnon Fair, Llanfairfechan items and people bewitched could be bathed in the waters of the well to be freed of the evil influence.[11]

Cattle who had fallen ill as the result of black witchcraft, could be taken to the Somerset well of St Aldhelm, to receive the blessing of the waters.[12]

---

10. Ibid, p. 86.
11. Bord, Janet. Cures and Curses – *Ritual and Cult at Holy Wells*, p. 31.
12. Ibid, p. 68.

There were also wells whose powers provided a preventative protection against ill-wishing and black witchcraft. Clouties were employed within such protective rites at some Irish wells where, after being affixed upon a thorn branch, the rag was spat upon. This, it was believed, protected people, as well as their cattle, from the influence of witchery and the mischief of the faery folk.

The Black Isle Craigie Well also had protective as well as prophetic powers. Upon the first Sunday in May, its water was at its most powerful in providing a protection against witchery, spirits and illness. Here, offerings of coins, clouties and locks of human hair were left.

Pins were thrown into a holy well at Rorrington, Shropshire, for good fortune and as a protection against witches.[13]

❧ Weather Magic ❧

Whilst the holy well at times served as a locus for rites of popular magic against the influences of witches and the faery; both have themselves been closely connected with wells as suitably liminal and potent places of dwelling, meeting or operating. In popular thought, the activities of witchcraft were closely associated with the weather, particularly with storms that blighted crops or wrecked ships; the blame for which was often laid at the witch's door. It was at wells that witches might perform their rites of conjuration to influence the weather.

This was not always to bring disaster upon her neighbours for, like Drake, legend tells that she might employ such well magic in defense against invaders by sea. At Sennen Cove at the far west of Cornwall, there was once a holy well and Chapel Idne, which legend tells us

---

13. Ibid, p. 145.

were the location of a witch rite performed by a woman to conjure 'a west wind' to thwart a Danish invasion. Her rite involved emptying the well, and sweeping the chapel with a broom.[14]

The weather magic performed by witches at holy wells could be of benefit to sailors. Weather rites were performed by witches at holy wells on the Isle of Man, in order to conjure useful winds which they would sell to sailors tied into three knots within a rope. In 1658, a suspected witch, Elizabeth Black, was accused of conjuring forth a 'favourable wind' by emptying a well until dry.[15]

'Sea Witches' along the north coast of Devon and Cornwall, Cecil Williamson tells us, would sell the wind to sailors in this fashion via the thrice knotted rope. One such Cornish 'sea witch' was Kate 'The Gull' Turner (1888 – 1961) of Penryn. In addition to providing divinations to seafaring folk, the Museum of witchcraft was informed by her granddaughter that Kate was known to 'sell the wind' to Penryn Sailors.

In Cornwall, witches are heavily associated with the folklore of 'wrecking', the practice said once to have been employed to deliberately cause shipwrecks in order that a community might benefit from the spoils of the doomed vessels as they were washed ashore by the tide. On Agnes, one of Cornwall's Isles of Scilly, is the holy well of St Warna – patroness saint of shipwrecks. Offerings were left at the well to encourage storms that might give up a good bounty to the islanders.[16]

In acts of 'sympathetic magic' water was a necessity within acts of witchcraft designed to cause the

---

14. 44.

15. Bord, Janet. Cures and Curses – *Ritual and Cult at Holy Wells*, p. 152.

16. Straffon, Cheryl. *Fentynyow Kernow – In Search of Cornwall's Holy Wells*, p. 44.

destruction of ships. In Scotland, witches would conduct such grim operations with a large vessel of water, upon which they would float a representative of the victim ship. This might be an actual model ship, or even just a small piece of wood. Chants of storms and destruction would be made as the 'image' of the ship was turned over, thus representing the capsizing of the actual target of their working.[17]

On the Isle of Skye, an apparent rite of shipwrecking was observed being performed by three witches. They had arranged a circle of black stones around the edge of the pool, and within it they had placed a cockleshell to float. The group was observed chanting an incantation until the cockleshell suddenly upended and sank to the bottom of the pool. It was believed that, as a result of this rite, a ship and all who were aboard it were mysteriously lost in calm and clear weather.

Other rites witch-covens were said to employ in order to conjure storms included beating the surface of water with wands; herein is a striking similarity to a Romany rite to bring forth rain which involved striking the surface of a pool with a stick of hazel.[18] If water was not available, the witches' own urine would suffice. Following this a special powder, given unto the coven by the Devil, was thrown up into the air and into the water. Via this, a strange cloud was raised forth which would produce a hail storm, and could be directed wherever the witches desired the hailstones to fall. Other rites for the same results included the act of digging holes in the earth, into which water or urine would be poured. A broom made wet by dipping its brush into water might be shaken to simulate a rain storm, sticks might be laid upon a dry river-bank, or a vessel of water might be set over a fire to boil, into which were placed either hog's bristles or eggs.

---
17. Howard, Michael. *Scottish Witches & Warlocks*, p. 152.
18. Kemp, Gillian. *The Good Spell Book*, p. 108.

The Magic of Springs & Holy Wells

Other storm conjurations didn't however require water; like the special Devil's powder, sea sand might be thrown into the air, or sacrificial pullets. The witches might also take up pieces of flint, stand with their backs to the west and toss the flints over their left shoulders, or sage leaves might be buried beneath the earth to rot.[19]

According to the extraordinary confessions of the Auldearn Witches in 1662, a rag dipped fully in water, and a 'cursing stone' were employed within storm conjurations. The stone was beaten with the wet rag with the thrice spoken charm: "I knock this rag upon this stone, to raise the wind in the Devil's name, it shall not lie until I please again." Thrice spoken also was the charm to lay the storm: "We lay the wind in the Devil's name. It shall not rise until we wish to raise it again."[20]

The North Berwick witches were said to have employed the sea itself in their cruel cursing rite designed to sink the ship carrying the king and his bride upon their return from Denmark. A cat had bound unto it the body parts of a dead man before being 'Christened' by the coven. The poor creature was thrown into the sea, causing the immediate conjuration of a severe storm. Whilst one ship was sunk, the king's ship just managed to stay afloat and return to Scotland safely.[21]

Returning to holy wells, weather magic was not the exclusive domain of witches, nor were seafaring folk entirely dependant upon witches for the conjuration of favourable winds. Matters concerning the weather formed a part of popular well magic; on the Hebridean island of Gigha, there was a well used by fishermen themselves to cast weather spells. The rite required that, after opening the well by removing its covering stones, the

---

19. Pickering, David. *Dictionary of Witchcraft*, p. 254-255.
20. Ibid.
21. Hole, Christina. *Witchcraft in Britain*, p. 15.

fisherman had to clean out the well using a clamshell, or a wooden dish. He then had to stand facing the direction he wanted the conjured wind to blow from, and throw the well's water a number of times in that direction with a spoken charm. Respect had to be paid to the well and its spirits in the careful replacing of the covering stones or a hurricane would instead be conjured.[22]

The fishermen of the westernmost Hebridean isle of St Kilda would go to a well to conjure a favourable wind by standing astride it each for a moment.[23]

Whilst the emptying of some wells was a method used by witches to conjure both tempests and favourable winds, the Inishmurray 'Well of Assistance', Tobernacoragh, could be used to calm storms by draining it into the sea.[24]

As the spirit of the well, engaged with ritually via either witchcraft or popular magic, will let forth the powers to conjure the conditions of weather desired, the neglect of holy wells could result in the withdrawal of beneficial weather essential for life. In the tradition of the well cult, the neglect of holy wells, and their spirits/saints, could signify a community's ignorance of the sacred and a tendency toward wicked profanity; a state of being with harsh consequences.

In Robert Hunt's Popular Romances of the West of England, we are told the legend of St Constantine's Well, St Meryn, Padstow. The people of the parish had gradually become quite irreverent and irreligious, as a result their church, chapel remains and holy well had become badly neglected; the well, being blocked with debris and weeds, became foul and stagnant. In punishment, a curse befell the people of the parish

---

22. Bord, Janet and Colin. *Sacred Waters*, p. 109.
23. Bord, Janet. Cures and Curses – *Ritual and Cult at Holy Wells*, p. 152.
24. Bord, Janet and Colin. S*acred Waters*, p. 109.

and nourishing rains ceased to fall with the arrival of a particularly hot and completely dry, long summer, and the rivers and streams ceased to flow. As the crops perished in the parched fields, the parish priest advised that the curse would be lifted if they would only repent and clear their sacred spring. They scorned the priest; believing the idea of clearing a filthy old well to bring rain was ridiculous. As their suffering continued, the priest again and again tried to convince the people of their error; "Cleanse the well, wash, and drink" he told them, until, in desperation, they went to the well. Here, they pulled away the weeds and debris, dug away the mud and silt until, to their amazement, a steady flow of crystal clear waters came forth in abundance. From it they drank, in it they bathed and prayed, and the skies clouded over and rains returned to give life and rich verdancy unto the land again.

For Love & Marriage

In occult thought, water is the allegorical emblem of the essence or element of being relating to the stillness or turmoil of emotion, empathy, the depth of memory, omniscience and verity. Those things corresponding with the essence of water may thus be of use within traditional magical operations of love and union, and as we have found, the popular divinatory uses of water and holy wells often related to matters of love.

There were holy wells that, rather than providing prophecies of love and matrimony, would be resorted to by those who sought, by aid of the spirits or 'saints', to bend fate to their will where marriage was concerned. Young women would visit the Somerset well of St Agnes on the night of the 20th of January; the eve of the saint's day. There, in the darkness of night, the young woman would whisper her desires of marriage over the waters in the hopes that, if the saint agrees, the maid shall have her husband within the year.[25]

The associations between sacred waters and matters of the heart and of verity are exemplified in the use of wells within poignant acts of pledge making, oath taking, swearing fealty and binding by one's word. Thus were holy wells visited by couples for the sealing of matrimonial engagement, or by married couples to pledge their eternal fealty and love for each other. One such pledging well was near the summit of Golfa Hill, Mid Wales. To Trinity Well, couples would make their way on Trinity Sunday and, in strict silence, would fill a cup from the well, mixing in a little sugar. From this same cup, both would drink in loving compact.[26]

Sadly, of course, rather than true equality in partnership, many seek mastery in marriage; a position a certain Cornish well was able to confer to the first of a newly married couple who drank the waters of the well following their wedding ceremony. An inscribed slate plaque, standing a little above the well of St Keyne, relates to the visitor the story of the well's power: "Saint Keyne was a princess who lived about 600 AD. She laid on the waters of this well a spell thus described by Carew in 1602 AD – 'The quality that man or wife whom chance or choice attains first of this sacred spring to drink thereby the mastery gains.'"

Being the first to drink of the waters of St Keyne, however, did not necessarily mean being the first to reach the well after the wedding ceremony, as revealed in the poem about the well by Robert Southey (1774–1843): "…I hastened, as soon as the wedding was done, and left my wife in the porch; but i'faith she had been wiser than me, for she took a bottle to church."

---

25. Bord, Janet. Cures and Curses – *Ritual and Cult at Holy Wells*, p. 141.
26. Ibid, p. 107.

The Magic of Springs & Holy Wells

~ Fertility Magic ~

Many holy wells and sacred springs were reputed never to run dry, even in times of severe drought; strengthening belief in the magical powers, or divine virtues of the well. In such times, the holy well, set within a parched and barren landscape would be an oasis of verdant life, thus exemplifying the power of the well to exorcise sterility and promote fecundity.

On the eve of the wedding day, the Aberdeenshire bride seeking to increase her fertility might visit the Bride's Well with her maids. There they would perform a rite in which the bride's maids would bathe her feet and upper body. Before leaving, the bride would offer unto the well a small amount of bread and cheese, to ensure that the family she hoped to begin would never go hungry.[27]

A more complex women's fertility rite, performed in complete silence, had been observed in secret by an Aberdeenshire boy who hid in the bushes beside a well in the mid 19th century. The rite was presided over and lead by an elderly woman for three young women who wished to conceive. The four women assembled around the well, the elderly woman went to her knees upon a stone beside it as the three young women undressed their bottom halves and rolled up their skirts to expose their abdomens. The old women directed the three to begin circumambulations about her and the well in the direction of the sun three times. With each pass, the old woman took up water from the well to splash upon their abdomens. Signalling to the young women to stop, she directed them to undress their top halves, exposing their breasts, and to kneel opposite her across the well. Again the old woman took up the waters and splashed it upon

---

27. Ibid, p. 46.

their breasts three times each. The four women arose, the three young women re-dressed and all departed from the well without a word being uttered.[28]

Barren women on the Isle of Man would perform fertility rites at the well of Chibbyr Unjin. Here the woman had to lay herself down and take a mouthful of the water. This had to be held within the mouth as she arose to circumambulate the well three times with the sun. The water was then spat out upon a cloutie which was hung upon a thorn branch.[29] This now destroyed well was believed to be at its most potent on St John's Eve.

The waters of a holy well might also be used to protect or promote the fertility of the land. In an interesting synthesis of pagan and Christian folk magic, lead ampullae brought by pilgrims from walsingham were found to have been deliberately buried in various parts of England at field boundaries. This appears to have been part of magical rites to encourage and protect the growth of crops, and one of the ampullae, when opened, was found to have had herbs as well as water sealed within it.[30]

ᦓ Holy Wells & Baptism ᦓ

We, born to God at the font, are children of the water.
Robert Stephen Hawker (1803 – 1875)

Within the ancient rites of baptism, we find exemplified not only water's washing away of impurity, or sin, but also its use within ritual to mark one as separate, initiated

---

28. Bord, Janet and Colin. *Sacred Waters*, p. 52.

29. Ibid, p. 82.

30. Bord, Janet. Cures and Curses – *Ritual and Cult at Holy Wells*, p. 33-34.

and brought into the protection and light of the divine. Veiled also within baptism, we find the themes of death and spiritual rebirth or resurrection; characteristic also of initiatory rites.

In ritual immersion, one is placed beneath the waters in death – removed from this world into the 'Other', then to be drawn up again from the depths into rebirth. The 'old self', its cares, impurities and 'sins' are by this death washed away, and the initiate is reborn unto divine illumination.

Cognate with this theme of new life is the creative act, exemplified in symbolism. Within the initiatory baptismal rites of varied traditions we find the conjunction of the waters of life with the sign of the cross; herein is the creative union of the feminine waters with the solar cross from which spiritual rebirth is engendered.

Whilst the holy well itself has long been the locus for baptismal rites, such as at Madron Well, where baptisms until relatively recently were conducted in early May, the church rites of Christening, often employed the waters of the holy well, sometimes at some distance from the church itself, which were drawn forth and poured into the font; there to be blessed as 'holy water'.

Cornish holy wells from which water was drawn for church Christening include Anne's Well Whitestone, St. Clether's Well, St. Johns well Morwenstow, Laneast Well, Michaelstow Holy Well, Holy Well of Our Lady of Nants, Blisland Holy Well and St. Pratt's Well.

In addition to formally bringing the child into the Church, there were also strong folk-magical elements to the rites of Christening and baptism in popular belief. The rite was believed to offer the child some protection against supernatural harm directed via the influences of witchcraft, the evil-eye, spirits and demons, as well as from illness and disease.

In traditional East Anglian belief, a child is thought unlikely to thrive until it has been baptised. If the child

Wisht Waters

becomes ill, the rite of baptism was believed to restore the child unto health.[31] Thus in some cases it was an operation of preventative and curative folk-magic.

In Romany belief, a newborn child is at great risk of falling to supernatural harm until it is named and ritually sprinkled with salt water.[32]

Objects might be ritually endowed with magical power by the Church via baptism. The Catholic rite of a bishop ceremonially baptising a bell with holy water, was to invest in the bell the powers to exorcise evil spirits, the Devil and storms by its ringing.[33]

---

31. Gurdon, Eveline Camilla (Ed.). *Old Suffolk Love and Cure Charms*, p. 14.
32. Buckland, Raymond. *Gypsy Witchcraft and Magic*, p. 11.
33. Bord, Janet. Cures and Curses – *Ritual and Cult at Holy Wells*, p. 12.

The Magic of Springs & Holy Wells

The Baptised Would Never Hang

A specific magical protection that some wells conferred upon those baptised by their waters, was protection from the hangman's noose.

In Cornwall, at the foot of Carn Brea Hill is to be found one such well; that of St Euny. Another is the well of St Ludgvan attached to which is a legend regarding this particular protective virtue. The land was dry, and so the saint prayed for water whilst kneeling upon the church stile. Immediately there issued forth from the earth a spring of crystalline clarity. Bathing his eyes within its water, he discovered that the power of his sight was at once rendered many times more powerful than it had ever before been. Drinking of its waters, he found his power of speech greatly refined, and he prayed over the waters that any child baptised from the spring shall never face the hempen noose and so the spring was thus empowered. Word spread of the new well's powers, and so it was not long before the first child was brought for baptism. During the ceremony, conducted by the saint, the young babe received from the water the power of speech, however, to the horror of all there assembled, each time the saint spoke the name of Jesus, the child would utter the name of the Devil. Evidently the child was possessed by an evil spirit and the saint immediately proceeded to perform exorcisms over the child, until, after a long struggle the spirit fled the child's body. The saint commanded the spirit to be bound unto the red sea, but, before leaving for its distant place of imprisonment, the spirit grew to an enormous stature, spat into the holy well and shook the pinnacles of the church tower, causing one to fall as he disappeared. By the spirit's desecration of the well, the water's powers over the eyes and speech had been destroyed; the power to save from the hempen noose miraculously remained.

Faith in this power too, however, was almost destroyed when a woman from Ludgvan, who had been convicted for murder, was sentenced to death and died by the hangman's noose. Faith was restored however when it was discovered, via the parish register, that this woman had not been baptised in St Ludgvan Church, and thus not in the waters of St Ludgvan's Well.

❧ *Desecration* ☙

Providing, as they have long done, a plethora of beneficial and useful virtues for employment by mankind, it is quite fitting that the holy well and sacred spring should also be possessed of the power to resist foolhardy molestation by humans, or to retaliate without mercy against it.

The stones of well structures, which at times might be removed, having caught the envying eye of those who would seek to remove them for more mundane uses, have been known to return by their own agency to their original positions. The stones of Cornwall's St Cleer's Well are said to have suffered various attempts to remove them, but in each case the robbed stones have been found mysteriously reinstalled in their proper place by morning.

St Nun's well of Pelynt is another Cornish well possessed of this same ability, but it is one that shall also retaliate with the utmost severity against its desecrators. Long serving as a dire warning is the story of a farmer who coveted the well's stone basin for a pigs' trough. Intent on claiming it, he fixed chains around the basin in order to pull it away from the well by his oxen and uphill to his awaiting wain. When almost there, the chains broke and the basin slid downhill, turning uncannily to reinstall itself in the well. Immediate and long lasting was the curse that the spirit of the well exacted in vengeance upon the farmer, for in an instant his oxen fell dead and he was struck lame and mute. A fairly wealthy man; his fortunes faded and he never prospered from that day.

Such was the fear people had for the retaliatory powers of holy wells, that when the squire desired to move the basin of St Cuby's Well in the mid 19th century, he was forced to agree pensions for the families of his workmen should any of them be killed by the spirit of the well during the basin's removal.[34]

---

34. Bord, Janet and Colin. *Sacred Waters*, p. 183.

The Magic of Pools, Ponds & Lakes

As with holy wells, areas of standing water are, in magical thought, representative of points of ingress or egress between the worlds, reflecting the fires of the heavens in their depths below and appearing as a mirror-like veil, barely concealing the Otherworld beyond. About such waters there often hangs a pervading sense that they are possessed of some strange and eerie intelligence; a palpable yet unfathomable presence; perhaps some primordial beast, fair 'Lady of the Lake' or deathly hag haunting the waters and its bounds.

Interaction with places and beings of liminality has always been sought by the magical practitioner in the hopes that, via such communion, the ways unto Otherworldly power and gnosis might be opened.

In Welsh tradition, one such practitioner was the celebrated 16th/17th century astrologer-wizard Huw Llwyd. Within the cascades of Cynfael, Cymorthyn, stands a colum of rock looking for all the world like a pulpit; indeed its name is Pulpud Huw Llwyd (Huw Llwyd's Pulpit), for it is from this rock the wizard is said to have performed his incantations by night, beside a pool deep and dark. Perhaps it was from a spirit of the waters that the wizard received his powers, for just as traditional belief holds that the witch cannot die until the powers he or she possesses are passed on, the wizard Huw Llwyd could not die until his books of the magical arts had been thrown into Llyn Pont, Rhyddu – 'the lake by the bridge of the black ford'. Upon his death bed, this task he gave unto his daughter, who desired to preserve her father's occult tomes and sought to conceal them. Her father, knowing that she had not completed her task, begged her until at last she did as she was bid. When, at the side of the lake, she threw her father's books, a mysterious hand arose from the water to catch them, and took them down beneath the surface and into the lake's depths.[35]

Pools, as we shall see, were of use with magical acts of such things as bindings and the breaking of bewitchments. One of the most interesting magical uses to which a pool might be put, for the general solving of a client's problems, was known to and employed by Cecil Williamson.

The operation, which must be performed upon a clear night, under a full moon, requires a pond, a large copper basin, a circular mirror, the urine of the client held within an earthenware jug, and the 'moon rake'. This intriguing object is a wooden pole, six foot in length and topped with a large iron shoe from a cart-horse. The witch begins by undressing their legs and feet so that they are able to step into the water of the pond, upon which they will set the copper basin to float with the mirror resting in its base. Gently guiding the basin, and holding the jug of urine, the witch will wade further into the pond until at knee's depth. Here, the witch shall empty the jug of urine into the basin, before making their way carefully back to land. Now the basin must be left to float as it will whilst the witch counts to sixty-six, after which the witch shall take up the moon rake. This is used as a tool to gently guide the basin into position so that its urine-submerged mirror reflects the light of the moon. Holding the basin in position via the moon rake,

---

35. Trevelyan, Marie. *Welsh Witchcraft, Charms and Spells*, p. 16-18.

the witch now employs what Cecil terms the 'thought-form-flow'. This is described as a silent conjuration in the mind the 'image' of the client's problem. Once this is formed, it is directed to flow down the shaft of the moon rake and into the urine within the basin. In this act, the witch should feel the pulse quicken, and a 'building up' to a surge and sudden 'emotional release'. The moon rake is then used to lift the basin out from the pond and placed carefully upon the ground. Here the witch pours the urine back into the jug before returning for home where the urine is to be boiled and then disposed of in a manner dependent upon the nature of the working, and the gender of the client.[36]

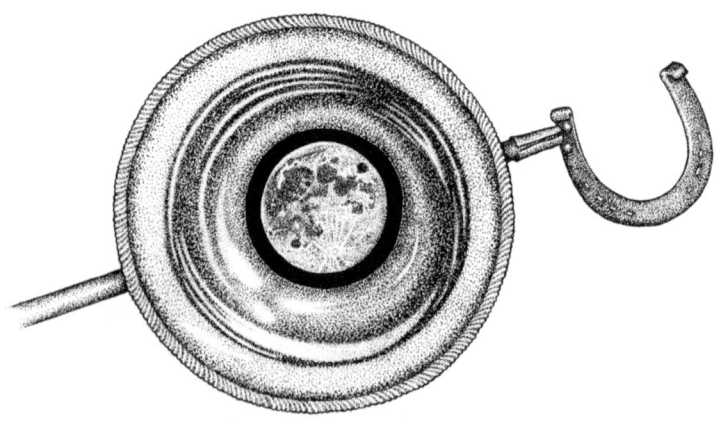

Against Bewitchments

Often, in dealings with a professional practitioner of magic, it was the client who would carry out the operations of a particular ritual, as directed by the practitioner consulted. In such arrangements however the scope for error is illustrated in the story of a Devonshire man who

---

36. Williamson, Cecil. *Dew Ponds, Moon-Raking & The Ritual of the Shroud, The Cauldron* No. 76.

had cause to believe himself 'overlooked'. The man, a farm-worker living near Exeter, consulted a 'white witch' who divined the identity of the one who was injuring him by ill-wishing. The culprit, so it was revealed, was the man's neighbour. To lift from himself the ill-influence, he was instructed to operate on the following night, before the moon arose by securing an article of his neighbour's clothing, bind it about a stone with string and throw it into the village pond. The next day, nervous of the task he was to undertake, he decided to visit the village inn to build a little courage until the time when the moon would soon be rising. Making his unsteady way from the inn, he proceeded to his neighbour's garden where clothing was still out on the line. Taking the first garment he caught hold of in the dark, he quickly did with it exactly what the white witch had directed and returned home relieved that he had been undiscovered in his activity. In the morning however, he awoke to a wife furious that her best chemise had been stolen – in his intoxication he had, the previous night, entered his own garden, and the garment now sitting at the bottom of the village pond was that of his wife![37]

The Binding of Spirits

Perhaps waters' liminality; the belief that it forms a boundary to the spirit world, and the taboos against seeing one's reflection in water for fear it should take something of one's soul relate to the old magical traditions of using bodies of water for the binding of troublesome spirits and possessed items in both clerical and folk-magical rites of exorcism?

The lonely Cranmere Pool on Dartmoor, which in reality exists in a liminal boggy state betwixt water

---

37. Farquharson-Coe, A. *Devon's Witchcraft*, p. 13.

and land, is one such locus for the magical binding of unruly ghosts, around which various stories have grown. Cranmere's most famous bound spirit is 'Cranmere Binjy', who appears in life to have been Benjamin Gayer/Gear; a 17th century merchant and Mayor of Okehampton. One of a number of stories relating to his ghost tell of him dying in shame and guilt, after saving himself from financial ruin by taking money intended for charity. Haunted by his misdeed, his spirit became restless and an annoyance to the town. Twenty-three clergymen were convened to perform rites of exorcism. Eventually they succeeded in binding the spirit into the body of an unbroken colt. In order to lay the spirit in Cranmere Pool, a skilled horseman was brought in to ride the creature to the desolate spot. The horseman was given the Holy Sacrament to offer him some protection in his task, an unused bridle to place over the colt's head and instructions that he must not allow the animal to look back at any point during the journey to the pool. Just prior to reaching the pool the horseman must also slip from the colt's back. He followed the instructions given, and, slipping from the colt before Cranmere was reached, he observed as the colt carried on, and disappeared beneath the pool. Here, the spirit of Binjy was bound until he had completed the impossible task to weaving ropes from sand.

In another version of the story, Binjy had been found guilty of sheep-stealing and, apparently in corporeal form, was given the task of emptying Cranmere Pool with a sieve in punishment. Seeking a solution to his impossible task, he killed a sheep, lined the sieve with its skin and was able to empty the pool. For his attempt to cheat his way out of punishment Binjy was hanged on Hangingstone Hill and his spirit bound in Cranmere Pool to the eternal task of sand-rope weaving.

The colt story is applied to another of Cranmere's ghosts; the spirit of a wicked farmer who was troublesome

The Magic of Pools, Ponds & Lakes

to the people of Mary Tavy. Seven clergymen were convened, and by their rites they succeeded in transforming the farmer's spirit into a colt. The task of leading the haltered spirit to Cranmere was given to a young farm hand, who was instructed to let go of the animal as the pool was approached, and to return home without looking back. He completed the task, but could not resist the urge to look round as the spirit colt entered the pool aglow with blue fire. Before disappearing beneath the surface however, the spirit inflicted a kick to the boy's face; rendering him blind for life.

An alternative to the sieve and sheepskin story tells that the spirit 'Bingie' was bound to the pool by a conjurer, and given the task of emptying the pool with a sieve. Discovering a sheepskin on the moor, and lining the sieve, the spirit quickly emptied the pool, the waters of which flowed down the hill to drown Okehampton.[38]

The setting of what were intended to be impossible tasks appears to have been a common way in which West Country conjuring clergy and cunning folk laid, or bound, spirits in water.

In Cornwall's Dozmary Pool the spirit of the wicked magistrate Tregeagle was bound, and given the task of emptying the pool with a leaking limpet shell. He then appears to have been bound to the sea waters off Padstow, where his task was to weave ropes from sand. In miserable frustration, his ghostly moans and cries so disturbed the people of Padstow that he was again transferred, down to a cove of Land's End, there bound with the task of sweeping out the sands returned by every tide.[39]

A Devonshire pool-bound spirit is Weaver Knowles of Dean Prior. So dedicated was he unto his trade, that

---
38. Whitlock, Ralph. *The Folklore of Devon*, p. 54-55.
39. St. Leger-Gordon, Ruth E. *The Witchcraft and Folklore of Dartmoor*, p. 53.

after his death the spirit could not be kept from working his old loom. The vicar, being brought to exorcise the weaver's ghost, managed to lead it to the churchyard, here taking up a handful of graveyard dust and casting it over the spirit whereupon it transformed into a black hound. The spirit, trapped in bestial form, he lead to the deepest basin-pool of Dean Burn; there binding it to the task of emptying the pool, thereafter known as Hound's Pool, with a leaking nutshell.[40]

Haunted and bewitched items might also be exorcised and bound within pools. One such item terrorized a Crediton woodworker and his family. A neighbour, shortly before leaving the area, presented the man with a tin full of assorted nails which, given his trade, was gratefully received. However, when the day came that the last nail was used, the empty tin revealed itself to be in some manner possessed by troubling the family greatly. Wherever and no matter how securely it was kept, it would break out, fly about and roll around on the floor. Eventually the man went to consult a white witch, whereupon he was advised to take the tin at midnight to a deep pond on a moonless night, and there throw the thing into the middle. This the man did, and when the tin hit the pool's water, it issued loud hissing sounds, and despite being empty and sealed, sank immediately to the bottom.[41]

⁓ Discovering the Drowned ⁓

The strange and eerie presence that pervades many bodies of still water may often appear to be of a rather dark nature; for many pools and lakes to this day are no strangers to death. In such places human life appears to

---

40. Ibid, p. 54.
41. Farquharson-Coe, A. *Devon's Witchcraft*, p. 8.

be a sacrifice periodically demanded and taken. Where pools and lakes have claimed a life, there were methods of divination to be employed in order to locate the body of the drowned.

In 1936, the pool of Meldon Quarry near Okehampton had claimed a life, and the body could not be found. It was decided that the old method of 'singing for a drowned body' should be employed, and so an Okehampton choir was assembled by the waters edge, there to perform a service of prayer and singing. The body was finally recovered a week following the rite.[42]

Other methods for locating a drowned body required the floating of a loaf of bread. In some versions, the loaf had to be weighted with mercury. It was placed to float freely upon the surface, and would eventually sink when it was directly over the spot where the drowned body lay.[43] In Brittany, the loaf would have a lighted candle inserted into it and set upon the water's surface. It was believed that it would immediately float to, and stop over the place where the body would be found.[44]

Curative Uses

Just as pooled waters could be employed in the exorcism of spirits and bewitchments, they might also be employed in the exorcism of ailments. A Suffolk rite to cure seizures requires the sufferer to find a short stick, and to cut within it a notch for every seizure they have suffered. To this charm-stick, a stone is then to be bound and taken in strict secrecy to a pond. Here the device is to be thrown into the middle, and the sufferer

---

42. St. Leger-Gordon, Ruth E. *The Witchcraft and Folklore of Dartmoor*, p. 85.
43. Ibid.
44. Walker, Charles. *The Encyclopedia of Secret Knowledge*, p. 202.

is to depart without looking back, and they must tell no one of the operation.[45]

As well as lakes and ponds, much smaller pools of water, more akin to many of the holy wells, also have their curative uses. In Ireland, water which has collected within a Bullaun stone has often been employed within rites to cure warts, in much the same manner as those performed at 'wart-wells'. The roots of ancient beech trees often form large knots above ground, encompassing the trunk of the tree. Within the hollows of these ancient tangled roots, water sometimes collects and this was employed as a cure-water for the treatment of thinning hair and to promote thicker growth.

---

45. Gurdon, Eveline Camilla (Ed.). *Old Suffolk Love and Cure Charms*, p. 18.

The Magic of Flowing Waters

Cutting serpentine tracks across the landscape, forming potent visual boundaries, and sculpting deep valleys of chthonic numinosity; streams and rivers possess a strong sense of kinetic living force, and, what Devonshire Cunning Man Cecil Williamson would call 'spirit force'.

There exists a wealth of spirit-lore and magical tradition associated with flowing waters, indeed Cecil Williamson had a number of uses for streams in his own magical workings. To make 'Charm Water', Cecil advises that nine stones of white quartz should be taken from the bed of a running stream, taking care to disturb the water's flow as little as possible. A quart of water should be drawn from the stream, dipping the jug with the direction of the flow so as again to cause as little disruption as possible. The living motion of the waters has a vital 'spirit force', and by such observances, this force is harnessed within the collected stones and water.

A fire is then to be built in which the quartz stones can be heated until they are glowing red, at which point they must be dropped into the quart of water which may be bottled and kept for use, principally for curative purposes. To cure whooping cough, a wine-glass of charm water prepared in this manner would be given to the child for nine consecutive mornings.

Within such practices, perhaps we may find the employment of the transformative virtues of the moon, via the repeated appearance of the number nine. Perhaps also we may find the generative serpentine 'spirit force', via the harnessing of the water's flow, and the use of fire and red hot quartz stones; hissing serpent-fashion in their immersion.

Stones collected from the bed of a stream might also be employed directly in the working of cure-charms. These could be used in acts of 'stroking-magic' by rubbing or smoothing them over the skin of the patient on the afflicted part of the body.[46]

Water was also employed by Cecil in his use of image magic. In making a poppet, Cecil would collect water to represent the blood and fluids of the body. For efficacy, and reasons of sympathetic magic, this had to be running water, which Cecil would collect in an earthenware jug. As we shall see in the case of blood-charming, there is a strong folk-magical correspondence between flowing water and blood. When image magic was employed in acts of cursing, part of Cecil's practice involved 'drowning' his poppets in water.

Blood-Charming

When charmers, possessed of the ability to stem the flow of blood, are called to charm the wounds of humans and animals, the method used often involves a spoken charm, sometimes written, invoking Christ's baptism in the River Jordan. Of this charm, many examples and slight variations exist, of which the following two West Country versions are quite typical:

> *Jesus was born in Bethlehem, baptised in the River Jordan, when the water was wild in the wood, the person was just and good, God spake and the river stood, and so shall thy blood, in*

---

46. Pickering, David. *Dictionary of Witchcraft*, p. 278.

The Magic of Flowing Waters

the name of the Father, the Son, and the Holy Ghost. Amen, Amen, Amen.

Christ our Lord was born in Bethlehem. He was baptised in the River Jordan. The waters ran rude. He bid it to stand and it stood. So shall the blood of (patient's name) be still, in the name of the Father, and the Son and the Holy Ghost. Amen. Praise God may all things pass away.

Within these charms, a sympathetic link is drawn upon between the flowing waters of the river, and the flow of blood from the patient's wound. The power of God, or of Christ, to still the river is invoked within the charm to halt bleeding. It is due to the sympathetic correspondence between the divine stilling of the waters, and the charmer's stilling of a bleed, that tradition maintains that the blood-charmer must not cross running water following the treatment of their patient. Upon their return home, a blood charmer would make great detours if necessary to avoid crossing a stream or river, otherwise blood would again start to flow forth from their patient's wound.[47]

Within this observance, we may find something of the old tradition that magic, spirits, witches and the like, cannot cross running water. Perhaps the crossing of a stream by a blood-charmer would result in the breaking of their 'spell'.

⁓ Other Cure Charms ⁓

Within a Welsh charm for ague, the sufferer had to observe the avoidance of crossing streams and rivers. With out crossing water, the sufferer had to go to a hollow willow tree. Into the trunk's hole, they would have to breathe

---

[47]. St. Leger-Gordon, Ruth E. *The Witchcraft and Folklore of Dartmoor*, p. 169.

three times before stopping up the opening as quickly as possible. The place would be left, without looking back, or a single word having been spoken.[48]

The potent living spirit force of particularly fast-flowing flowing streams could be harnessed for curative purposes, simply by applying their water to the afflicted parts of the patient. In this manner, many ailments, including sciatica, thrush and warts could be treated.[49]

Streams held an important place in the rich corpus of rites employed in Romany tradition. For curative purposes, upon either a full or new moon, an ailing person could be taken to a stream, wherein their hands and face would be bathed to 'wash' the illness away.[50] For the same purpose, nail parings and hair clippings from the ailing person might be cast into a stream to carry the affliction away.[51]

A Romany cure for cramps involves simply gathering water from a stream, placing it in a bowl and keeping it beneath the bed. The presence of this water will bring relief to the sufferer who sleeps over it.[52]

To aid the teething process, Welsh Gypsies would give the child stream-water to drink from a thimble. Gypsies in Transylvania would employ streams to cure toothache. A barley straw would be bound around a stone which was to be thrown into a stream with a spoken charm: "Oh, pain in my teeth trouble me not so greatly! Do not come to me, my mouth is not thy house. I love thee not at all; stay away from me. When this straw is in the brook, go away into the water."[53]

---

48. Trevelyan, Marie. *Welsh Witchcraft, Charms and Spells*, p. 21.
49. Pickering, David. *Dictionary of Witchcraft*, p. 278.
50. Kemp, Gillian. *The Good Spell Book*, p. 49.
51. Ibid, p. 44.
52. Ibid, p. 53.
53. Buckland, Raymond. *Gypsy Witchcraft and Magic*, p. 61.

Protective Uses

In addition to acts of blood-charming, the Divine stopping of the waters of the River Jordan might also be invoked within other forms of binding spell. In Suffolk it was invoked within a spell to bind potential assailants: "Whoever thou art that meanest me ill, stand thou still! As the river Jordan did when our Lord and Saviour, Jesus, was baptised therein. In the name of Father, Son, and Holy Ghost. Amen."[54]

The potent boundary that flowing waters formed in traditional belief; forbidding the crossing of magic, spirits, witches and other beings of a supernatural nature, have caused it to occupy a similar position in such belief to that of the cross-roads. Beneath the beds of streams and rivers, just as at crossroads, burials of executed criminals, suicides and suspected vampires would take place in the belief that the barrier of flowing water would prevent the rising and wandering of their ghosts.[55]

Beliefs surrounding water as a protective barrier against malevolent supernatural agencies may be found in the tradition of leaving a bowl of water outside the door to the house over night. Such would serve the dual function of pleasing the 'good folk', and guarding the house from spirit intrusions of a harmful nature.[56] It was because of the protective influence the presence of water had against evil spirits, that it was traditionally considered unwise to throw water out of the house after dark.[57] The hearth, being a vulnerable point of spiritual ingress into the household, was a traditional place for a

---

54. Gurdon, Eveline Camilla (Ed.). *Old Suffolk Love and Cure Charms*, p. 30.
55. Pickering, David. *Dictionary of Witchcraft*, p. 278.
56. Whelan, Edna. *The Magic and Mystery of Holy Wells*, p. 83.
57. Pickering, David. *Dictionary of Witchcraft*, p. 278.

variety of protective charms. Here too waters would be kept, both as an offering to beneficial household spirits, and as a barrier to ill-influence.

∽ Against Witchcraft & the Evil-Eye ∾

The hearth was also guarded by the application of water in Scottish folk-magical rites to cure those suffering illness as a result of being 'overlooked'. Where a pool had formed in a river beneath a bridge leading to a churchyard, over which 'the dead and the living pass', water would be collected and taken to the victim of the evil-eye. The water was held within a ladle of wood, into which a piece of silver had been placed. From this, the patient would sip thrice during the recitation of a charm. Around the patient and at his hearth, the remainder of the water would be sprinkled.[58]

A rite to lift the influence of the evil-eye, that Raymond Buckland tells us he once saw performed in Cornwall by an elderly Romany witch, involved the use of stream water. She had filled a bottle from a stream, and added some salt. Her patient, a girl who had been 'overlooked' was instructed to remove her clothes and lay upon the ground with her head to the east. The witch stood at the girls head for some time, before circumambulating about her with the sun, reciting a charm and between each line she would take a mouthful from the bottle, then allowing the salted water to trickle from her mouth onto her patient's body.[59]

To cure children and protect children from the evil-eye, a Romany spell might be performed by going to a stream, there to let its current fill a jar. Later, to this jar of stream water, seven cloves of garlic, and seven pieces of coal are to be added and left for seven days. The content

---

58. Bord, Janet & Collin. *Sacred Waters*, p. 67.
59. Buckland, Raymond. *Gypsy Witchcraft and Magic*, p. 94.

of the jar is then to be emptied into a pot and set to boil over a fire, being stirred with a three-forked stick. When this charm-water has cooled, the stick is used to flick it seven times over the child.[60]

Another version of this spell is given by Raymond Buckland as being one employed by Continental Gypsies. A kettle is taken to a stream and filled with the water's flow, not against it. To the stream-filled kettle are added seven pieces of coal, seven handfuls of meal, and seven garlic cloves. The kettle is then brought to the boil and stirred with a three-forked stick as a charm is spoken: "Evil eyes that look on thee, may they here extinguished be! And then seven ravens pluck out the evil eyes. Evil eyes now look on thee, may they soon extinguished be! Much dust in the eyes, so may they become blind. Evil eyes now look on thee, may they soon extinguished be! May they burn; may they burn, in the fire of all good!" [61]

When a child is suspected of having been 'overlooked', the Romany mother might go to a stream, holding the child over the water with its face as close as possible to the flowing surface. As she does so a charm is spoken: "Water, water, hasten! Look up; look down. Let as much water come into the eye that looked evil on thee. May it now perish." If the child has been inflicted by the evil-eye, then the sound of the stream will become louder.[62]

Divinatory Uses

Charles Godfrey Leland tells us that a human baby might also be taken to a stream for the performance of

---

60. Kemp, Gillian. *The Good Spell Book*, p. 49.
61. Buckland, Raymond. *Gypsy Witchcraft and Magic*, p. 93.
62. Ibid.

a Romany rite of divination, following the theft of a horse. To discover in which direction the stolen horse has been taken, the child is held over the stream with a spoken charm: "Tell me, O Nivaseha, by the child's hand, where is my horse? Pure is the child; pure as the sun, pure as water, pure as the moon, pure as the purest. Tell me, O Nivaseha, by the child's hand, Where is my horse?"[63]

There is a long tradition of witches, 'wise-women' and cunning men along London's River Thames, the waters of which would be employed in a number of divinatory methods. Some of the magical practitioners living and working along the river's banks could make divinations by reading the waters as their colours changed throughout the seasons. During these divinatory rites, we are told that the practitioner must maintain a calm and peaceful state for the operation to have any efficacy.

Other Thames magicians would divine by 'water gazing'. A deep trance-like state would be achieved as the diviner stared into the river's surface, therein to see images and visions arising from the depths.

Rather akin to some of the popular methods of divination employed at holy wells, by dropping in pebbles or pins to count any resulting bubbles, some Thames diviners would make use of pebbles. These would be thrown into the river, and divinations made by counting the number of resulting ripples.[64]

Matters of Love & Fertility

Like holy wells, streams were also places for the making of oaths and compacts. To seal their love for one another, a

---

63. Ibid, p. 141.
64. Latimer, Simon. *Witchcraft and Magic in London*, p. 17.

The Magic of Flowing Waters

couple would stand either side of a stream, holding hands over the flowing waters. Perhaps such an act calls upon the virtues of the stream as a spirit-barrier; invoking a protection from supernatural interference upon the couple's union?[65]

When, however, a Romany couple experience problems, and one of the partnership leaves, the other might go to a stream with one of their missing partner's shoes. Upon the shoe is written a wish before it is thrown into the stream to take the couple's problems away with it.[66]

In Romany tradition, we are told that a young woman desiring to become pregnant will visit a stream, bearing her 'snake beads'. She would have made these beads upon her first menstruation; mixing her blood with clay to make a set of beads. These 'snake beads', or 'sap beads', form a charm protecting against pregnancy. However, when a child is desired, the young woman will go, alone, to a stream and throw in the beads whilst making a wish for pregnancy. Power for many other purposes may be worked into clay beads by Romany witches, later to be released by allowing them to dissolve in water.[67]

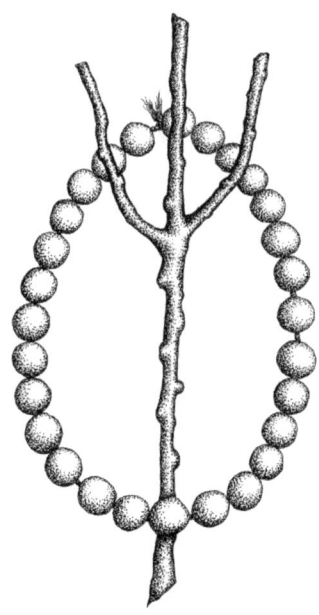

⁓ Sacrifice ⁓

There are rivers, believed to be possessed of some ancient spirit, that require periodical sacrifice; often that of a human life. One such river, laden with

---

65. Bord, Janet & Collin. *Sacred Waters*, p. 108.
66. Kemp, Gillian. *The Good Spell Book*, p. 29.
67. Buckland, Raymond. *Gypsy Witchcraft and Magic*, p. 135.

traditions of demanding human life, is the Devonshire River Dart. About the river there are sayings: "Dart, Dart, cruel Dart, every year thou claim'st a heart." And "Dart, Dart, Wants a Heart."

There is also the tradition of 'The Cry of the Dart'. At times, the Dart is productive of unusually loud noises, which in old belief was the spirit of the river calling for its next heart.[68]

Also in Devonshire, Kingsteignton's annual ram-roast feast, held at Whitsun, is associated with traditions of river sacrifice. It has also been suggested that the feast is a survival of pagan festival sacrifices for fertility.[69]

In one story associated with the feast, a baptism needed to be performed urgently, however, the village was suffering a terrible drought and there was no water available to perform the rite. A ram was taken to the dry riverbed and there sacrificed, whereupon water began to arise from the earth until the river again flowed. As the child was baptised in its waters, the skies let forth rain upon the village.[70] In another version of the story, when drought struck the village, its priests petitioned the gods, and they answered be setting the stream aflow again. In gratitude to the gods, a ram lamb was sacrificed.[71]

---

68. St. Leger-Gordon, Ruth E. *The Witchcraft and Folklore of Dartmoor*, p. 87.
69. Ibid, p. 89-90.
70. Ibid.
71. Whitlock, Ralph. *The Folklore of Devon*, p. 128.

The Magic of the Sea

The sea shore is a truly liminal place; a meeting of worlds where the immense power of the tides shape and erode the seeming solidity of land. From the sea, storms appear to be born forth to the ride across the earth, and from it the sun itself seems to arise from and return in setting to the underworld; a giver of birth and receiver in death. It is a place of magic, where the powers of change and transformation may be invoked and harnessed via the eternal ebb and flow of the tides of sea and moon.

The power of tide was employed within the magical work of Cecil Williamson. What ever it was that required banishment, be it an illness or some other undesirable situation, a knot charm could be employed by tying knots, as many as there are troubles, or aspects to the trouble, into rope, cord or string, and touch these each to the thing to be banished, or a symbol thereof. The knot charm is then taken to the shore where it is buried at the mark of low water. The operator will then walk away and must not look back or catch sight of the spot for at least twentyfour hours.

When it was suspected in the Outer Hebrides that a child was a changeling, the tide would be employed to return the human child from the Otherworld. To just below the high water mark, at low tide, the child is taken and there left upon the sand, paying no heed to its cries and screams. It is hoped that the faery will not allow one of their young to be drowned by the incoming waters, and will take it away, leaving the human child in its place. The success of the operation was indicated if the changeling, identified by its incessant screeching, should suddenly become quiet.[72]

For Safety at Sea

Most traditional labours, crafts and trades have their concomitant superstitions, rites and charms, and of these, protections from danger are prime motivators. Thus, occupations of a particularly hazardous nature, such as fishing and seafaring, are attended to by a wealth of magical protections.

Items from the sea itself often were employed as protective charms, notably various kinds of fossils, which have long been regarded as particularly mysterious items, each with their own attached folklore. The 'Aristotle's Lantern', which is from the mouth parts of Echinoids or Sea Urchins, was carried as a protective charm against drowning in Jersey, and for the same reason the 'teeth'

---

72. Henderson, William. *Witchcraft, Toadlore and Charms of the Northern Counties*, p. 11.

The Magic of the Sea

from Aristotle's Lanterns were carried as charms in Normandy and Brittany.[73]

A number of fish-bone charms were collected by Cecil Williamson for his Museum of Witchcraft. Of these, four are triangular bones carried by fishermen as protective charms against storms at sea, as well as thunder and lightning. These were obtained from a St Ives sea witch. Another fish bone in the collection is in the form of a Tau cross, believed to have been an amulet against drowning.

Also in the collection are two charms made from lobster claws, with metal mounts for hanging. One of these, an example from Mevagissey, we are told was provided by a sea witch who would have concealed a written charm within the claw, and was to be suspended from a ceiling hook in the cabin of a crabber. Such a charm, it was believed, would protect craft and crew, as well as promoting good catches. The other example is from Italy, and was acquired by Gerald Gardner.

Items such as 'sea beans', having floated in across the seas from more 'exotic' locations, would also have been viewed as 'strange' and perhaps possessed of some magical power. In the Museum of Witchcraft we find the seeds of the Mucuna plant, known in many places as 'Horses' Eyes', which find their way from Central and South America to Northern European shores. One such sea bean, in the Clarke collection at Scarborough Museum, was collected from the Hebrides where it was kept as a charm against drowning.

Interestingly, bones from creatures not of the sea were also employed as charms against drowning. Two such examples, also in Scarborough Museum, consist of a fowl's wishbone and called a 'merrythought' used

---

73. Cadbury, Tabitha. *The Clarke Collection of Charms and Amulets, Museum of Witchcraft Archive.*

by South Devon sailors, and the hyoid bones of sheep carried as charms by Scarborough fishermen.

Also, in the 19th century, it had been noted that the wives of Scarborough sailors were in the habit of keeping black cats within their homes. To do so, they believed, would ensure the safety of their husbands whilst at sea. [74]

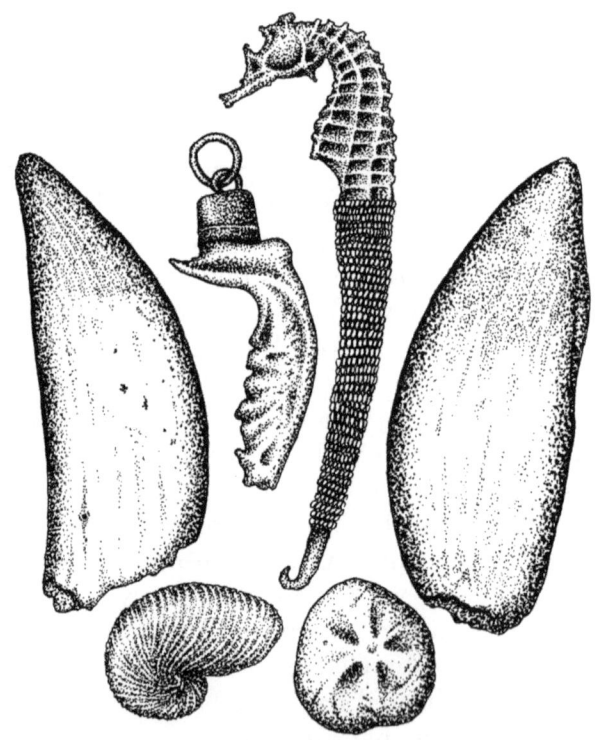

The most potent and highly sought-after amulet against drowning at sea appears to have been the child's caul, or

---

74. Henderson, William. *Witchcraft, Toadlore and Charms of the Northern Counties*, p. 29.

*'*birth cap*'*. An example of a child's caul amulet may be seen in the Museum of Witchcraft, Boscastle, and two examples are in the Scarborough Museum collection. We are told that the 'wise-woman midwife' was in an ideal position to obtain these much coveted membranes, which may envelope a child's head at birth. These she would be able to sell, for high prices, to fishermen and sailors, for it was the old belief that anyone who possessed such an item would never die by drowning.

One caul, in the Clarke collection at Scarborough Museum, is held within a leather bag, whereby it could be worn about the neck. It was kept by Skipper John Cave, from 1830 to 1870, whereupon it was inherited by his son, remaining in his keeping until 1926.

Other Protections

Seahorses; those strange and beautiful creatures, Otherworldly in their movements, would, in their appearance, be at home amongst the wonderful and bizarre entries in a medieval magical bestiary. They seem to have been employed in many parts of the world as charms and amulets against the evil-eye. Dried specimens might be carried, or hung within the home, sometimes with the incorporation of tiny glass beads, which have their own tradition of use in the averting of evil. The image of the seahorse, made from glass might also be employed in this manner, as would images of fishes, also in glass or Mother-of-Pearl.

Bones and parts of actual fish were also possessed of amuletic properties. The skull of an unknown fish with attached vertebrae in the Museum of Witchcraft, bares the natural image of a crucified figure within its form; suggesting, as other natural manifestations of cross-forms do, a magical, protective use. Scarborough Museum houses a pair of otoliths or 'ear stones' from a codfish, which were worn by women within charm-bags as a protective against conception.

Items resembling eyes, by obvious reasons of sympathetic magic, have always been employed as charms to ward off the influence of the evil-eye, and such items coming from the sea might be believed particularly efficacious. The operculum (foot-closure) of sea molluscs, might possess eye-like and spiralling markings, and would be carried as charms. Some had names such as 'cat's eyes', or 'Eye of St Lucia'.

Various kinds of animal heart, stuck with such things as thorns, nails or pins, are to be found within the folk-magical counter measures against 'black witchcraft'.

Within Scarborough Museum's Clarke collection of charms we find, collected from South Devon, the heart of a seagull, stuck with pins to exorcise the influence of malefic magic.

Sea fossils, as well as guarding against drowning, had other protective uses. The fossils of sea urchins, or Echinoids, were employed for a variety of protections. Upon these fossils, one might find a star-like pattern, very reminiscent of the 'daisy-wheels', which one might find inscribed into the timbers and masonry of ancient buildings, most likely for apotropaic purposes.

Their folk names include shepherd's crowns, thunder stones and fairy loaves. They protected against thunder, evil spirits and witches, prevented milk turning sour, and in common with other fossil amulets, they sweated in the presence of poison. As 'fairy loaves' they might be used to ward off supernatural interference from the baking process, and to ensure an abundance of bread.

Belemnite fossils, from an extinct squid-like creature, were known as thunderbolts, and were thus kept as charms to protect against lightning. Once believed to be the tongues of ancient serpents, fossilised shark teeth were one of the fossil amulets against poison.

Red coral has a long tradition of amuletic use against the evil-eye, particularly in Italy where it would be carved into apotropaic forms, such as horns and the Mano in Fica and Mano Cornuta gestures. Necklaces strung with red coral pieces were popularly worn for the same protective purposes.

A lump of coral in the Clarke collection was kept on Jersey as a charm against the Devil by being carried on the nights between Christmas and New Year.

Rings of stone, formed from the fossilised stems of the sea-lily were known as St Cuthbert's Beads, and were worn as amulets against evil influences.

Holed flints, known by various folk names, including hag-stones, witch-stones and holy-stones, are famous for their amuletic uses in many situations. In Devonshire, they would be affixed in the bows of boats to guard them from being 'overlooked' or 'witched'. The boat might also be protected from evil spirits by ensuring that such a stone were also affixed to the rope used to pull the boat ashore.

For Good Fortune

Gifts given of the sea might also possess the ability to encourage luck and good fortune. Coal is a traditional luck bringer; representing fuel for the hearth, thus prosperity and plenty. Sea-coal, found washed ashore by the tides, is a particularly fortunate find. A South Devon fisherman, visiting the Museum of Witchcraft, explained that it is traditional for such coal to be kept aboard fishing boats as an amulet of good fortune.

The dried eyeballs of codfish, and whelk shells, are revealed as other luck bringing amulets by the Clarke collection.

The 'Horse's Eye' sea-bean, in addition to its protective virtues, is also traditionally a bringer of good luck and fortune. In Scotland, they were sought and worn as magical attractors of prosperity. By virtue of its form and folk names, the mermaid's purse, or Devil's purse (the egg capsules of some sharks and skates), is suggestive of wealth, and would thus be employed as a household charm.

The cowrie shell, having a place within the folk beliefs of many parts of the world, is naturally suggestive both of eyes, and of the feminine. Thus at once it is both associated with averting evil, and with fertility and good fortune. As a household charm, large cowries might be kept upon the mantelpiece to promote good luck.

Fishermen of the Southeast Asian Island of Timor might also seek to harness the abundance attracting virtues of the cowrie, by affixing the shells to their fishing nets to promote good catches.

Other charms employed by fishermen seeking to encourage good catches may be found in Scarborough Museum and include ammonite fossils, worn by fishermen in Folkestone, and a 'Bollan Bone', a Ballan Wrasse's pharyngeal bone which was carried by fishermen on the Isle of Man. Most interesting of such charms is perhaps the full feathered skin of a kingfisher, which was nailed to the mast of a Guernsey fishing vessel, employed no doubt in magical sympathy with the bird's own fish-catching skills. The use of a hare's tail as a charm to attract abundant catches is perhaps less easy to fathom.

Ominous of catches however, was the appearance of a 'Butt Horn' – a starfish. If one were to be caught on the line of a Scarborough fisherman, the catching of a halibut was foretold.

❧ Healing & Cure-Charms ☙

Sea water itself is considered by many to have curative virtues, and that by bathing within it one might partake of some beneficial influence. To some, particular curative potency might be enjoyed by bathing in the sea 'while the books were open in church'.[75]

The apotropaic virtues of coral are in good company with its encouragement of fertility and benefits to health, which include the teeth and the prevention of sore throats when worn as necklaces by children.

The 'Devil's Toenail' fossils were carried as charms against rheumatic pain, and they were powdered to be used in the treatment of soreness of the back in horses.[76]

Other anti-rheumatic charms, given by the sea, include the stems of laminaria digitatum seaweed, carried by people in Scarborough, and carved pieces of amber, made and worn by Suffolk fishermen. The 'Horse's Eye' sea-bean makes an appearance again, for it was carried as an charm against rheumatism in Jamaica.[77]

❧ Sea Witches ☙

The vital need amongst sailors and fishermen to ensure safety, and to gain foreknowledge of the weather, has provided harbour-side magical practitioners and 'sea witches' with a healthy trade.

---

75. Bord, Janet. Cures and Curses – *Ritual and Cult at Holy Wells*, p. 135.

76. Examples may be found in The Museum of Witchcraft, and The Natural History Museum.

77. Cadbury, Tabitha. *The Clarke Collection of Charms and Amulets*, Museum of Witchcraft Archive.

Various accoutrements of the sea witch's divinatory work may be seen in the Museum of Witchcraft. Here we find that belemnites were employed by a Newlyn sea witch named Nancy. She would read the fall of her 'sea stones' to make predictions for fishermen. Perhaps their traditional associations with lightning gave belemnites the virtue to make predictions regarding storms and changes in the weather?

Cecil Williamson tells us that other sea witches made use of 'mermaid's combs'. These are the snouts of saw fishes, which the sea witch would use to rake line patterns in the sand upon which to cast such things as stones, shells and feathers to make readings from.

Housed also in the museum is the 'talking tambourine' which was employed within the divinatory work Kate 'The Gull' Turner (1888 – 1961), a sea witch of Penryn. Upon the underside of its skin are marked red lines, and a number of cowrie shells and 'Aristotle's Lanterns' would be placed upon it to move and change their positions as Kate drew her fingers along the other side of the skin. By the movements of these objects she would make predictions for her seafaring clients, to whom she was known also to sell the wind within knotted lengths of rope.

A sea witch, once living and working in Mevagissey, would perform magical workings by two 'tusks', which are in fact Sperm Whale teeth. These she would employ in acts of 'stroking magic' whereby she would stroke and smooth one of the 'tusks' whilst chanting the words of a spell. One of the 'tusks' was used for workings of a beneficent nature, the other for curse magic and blasting.

❦ *Spirit Binding* ❦

Whilst some clergy and magical practitioners might choose to bind exorcised spirits within pools, as we have seen in the case of Tregeagle, the sea was also employed.

The Magic of the Sea

The Red Sea was a favourite binding destination amongst some conjurers and cunning folk to send and bind spirits. One such Cornish practitioner was known as the Conjurer of St Colomb. Often he was called to exorcise houses believed to be haunted by the presence of evil spirits. In performing his exorcisms, he would employ a heavy stick, to beat upon the walls and furniture of the house whilst repeatedly declaiming loudly; "Out! Out! Out! Away! Away! Away! To the Red Sea, to the Red Sea, to the Red Sea!" This he would often follow with 'violent enunciation and much action, a torrent of incoherent and often incomprehensible words'.[78]

---

78. Hunt, Robert. *Popular Romances of the West of England.*

The Magic of Dew

The mysterious appearance of dew overnight, adorning all greenery, and hanging jewel-like upon silken webs made visible by its presence, is, in old belief, a magical occurrence. Arriving unseen, and without the fall of rain, dew has been thought to be the 'breath of god', or the manifest work of Ersa; daughter of the moon and of Zeus.

To this strange substance have been attributed various potent virtues and beneficial magical properties. Like the waters of many holy wells, the potency of Dew is traditionally at its zenith with May's arrival; for maximum efficacy, the dew had to be gathered at or before sunrise on the first of May.

Its most famed application is for clarity of complexion, whereby those who bathe their face in the May morning dew, will for the rest of the year enjoy a flawless complexion free of spots, freckles and other blemishes.

For such purposes it is suggested that efficacy can be increased further by collecting the dew from the leaves of the hawthorn, from the grass surrounding oaks, or from ivy leaves.

On the Isle of Man, the rite of bathing the face with the May morning dew had the added benefit of providing a protection against the influences of malefic witchcraft. [79]

---

79. Bord, Janet & Collin. *Sacred Waters*, p. 108.

The Magic of Dew

~ Curative Uses ~

The bringing of clarity of vision is another major traditional virtue of the dew. Arising in the early hours of the morning to bathe one's eyes with dew was believed to bring renewed power and clarity to one's sight, and to bring improvement to those suffering eye disorders such as cataracts.[80]

Pure rain water, collected in June within a clean vessel, was also employed as a curative for sore eyes. Kept within a bottle, such water would remain fresh indefinitely.[81]

In M.A Courtney's Cornish Feasts and Folklore, we find that the people of Launceston employed dew to cure swelling in the neck. Before sunrise on the 1st of May, the patient must visit a churchyard and there seek a particular grave. If the patient is a woman, she must go to the grave of the last young man to be interred there, whilst the male patient must find the last burial of a young woman. Here, the dew is gathered by thrice passing a hand from the head to the foot of the grave, and then applied to the affliction.

To treat a child afflicted with a weakness of the back, the May morning Dew is employed by taking the child out before sunrise on the 1st, 2nd and 3rd of May, where he or she is to be drawn over the dew moistened grass.[82]

In the late 1940's, witches on the Isle of Man gave Cecil Williamson a method of employing dew called 'The Ritual of the Shroud'. In a flat glen, a square cross-grid of twine is set up upon three foot high sticks, inserted into the ground. Upon this is pegged out a clean sheet of white linen, and there left overnight. The practitioners

---

80. Gurdon, Eveline Camilla (Ed.). *Old Suffolk Love and Cure Charms*, p. 17.
81. Bord, Janet & Collin. *Sacred Waters*, p. 108.
82. Courtney, M. A. *Cornish Feasts and Folklore*, 34.

of the rite must return to witness the dawn, before removing the dew saturated sheet and folding it into a basin and taking it to the awaiting client. Under a state of hypnosis, and remaining completely still, as though dead, the client is shrouded entirely with the sheet and bound with white cords, before being laid out upon a flat board bed. Here they are to remain until the warmth of their body has caused the dew to evaporate, leaving the shroud dry to the touch.

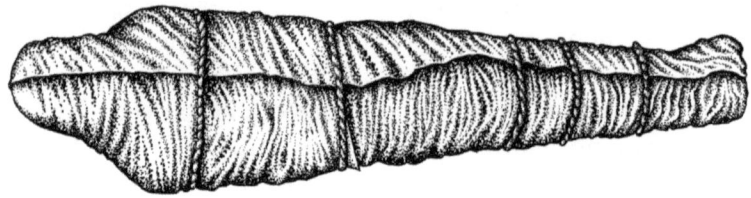

We also learn from Cecil that the wise-women of Dartmoor and Bodmin Moor, would venture out to gather the dew which channels and collects within the weather-worn basins of the granite rock piles and boulders of the moors. This they employed within their magical workings, to prepare their herbal medicines, and to administer curative pills and powders.[83]

A variation of the Launceston rite, Cecil knew of a dew gathering rite for use within image magic. The practitioner must go to a churchyard before sunrise on the 1st of May, and seek the graves of the most recently interred young man and young woman. From these, the dew is to be gathered by drawing a white cloth over the graves from head to food. The gathered dew is to be wrung out into a basin, and poured into a glass bottle, the dew from the two graves being bottled separately. Within workings of image magic, this grave

---

83. Williamson, Cecil. *Dew Ponds, Moon-Raking & The Ritual of the Shroud*, The Cauldron No. 76.

The Magic of Dew

dew may be used to ritually baptise and name the witch's images and poppets.

❧ Dew-Witching in the Pasture Fields ❧

Of the numerous methods that tradition holds were employed by witches in order to conjure milk, or to steal it from cows, one, apparently widely used, involved the gathering of dew. For this purpose, as with others, the dew is to be gathered before the rising of the May morning sun, and from the pastures used by the cows to be magically and absently milked.

The practice must have been particularly prevalent in Germany where an appellation for a witch is 'Daustriker', meaning 'dew-striker' or 'dew-scraper'.[84]

In Scotland, it is said that a farmer, out with his shotgun early on May Day morning found two elderly women, locally suspected of witchcraft, in the pasture fields. Here, they were brushing up the dew with a knotted rope of hair, which they dropped upon fleeing at realising their activity had been discovered. This device, the farmer took home, and placed above the cow-house door. Soon, the cows were yielding such quantities of milk, that the dairymaids could not find pales enough to take it. Only upon the witches' device being taken down and burnt did normality return to the dairy. In its burning, it is said the knots tied within the hair-rope each 'went off like a pistol-shot'.[85]

When a witch desired to steal butter from her neighbours, she might take up the dew from each of their pasture-fields with large sheets of linen. These she would wring out into a basin, to be transferred later

---

84. Henderson, William. *Witchcraft, Toadlore and Charms of the Northern Counties*, 21.
85. Ibid.

for keeping perhaps into a bottle. When she wished to conjure the butter, a spoonful of this May dew she would put into her churn with the words: 'From every house a spoonful'. From her churn thus would come a spoonful of butter from each of the owners of the pasture-fields she had harvested of May dew.[86]

In Pembrokeshire, before they are first put out to pasture, cows could be protected from bewitchment by tying rags and ribbons of red around their tails. Thus the cows would be guarded from the influence of witches who took up the dew from the pastures upon which they grazed.[87]

---

86. Ibid.
87. Trevelyan, Marie. *Welsh Witchcraft, Charms and Spells*, p. 5.

Charm-Waters

This is wonderfully good, and serveth excellently to excite and cause heavy rains, if it be engraved upon a plate of silver; and if it be placed under water, as long as it remaineth there, there will be rain. It should be engraved, drawn, or written in the day and hour of the moon. The Key of Solomon; The Sixth and Last Pentacle of the Moon.

Holy water, that which may be drawn forth from any source and made 'holy', and thus invested with power and spiritual virtue, via its blessing by a priest, has always been sought after and employed for various purposes within folk-magic.

Perhaps principally for its reputed powers of protection against evil, and its use to bless items within church services, holy water was taken from fonts for employment within 'unauthorised' acts of magic and rites of popular superstition. To prevent the removal of water for such uses, church authorities in the Middle Ages prescribed that font covers should be fitted with locks.

The folk-magician, witch, and practitioner of popular magic however, was never entirely reliant upon the priest, for there have been many ways to bless, consecrate and 'sain' water, thus rendering it more potent and useful within various rites and magical operations.

This might be achieved by steeping or immersing charmed items within the water, or else allowing water to flow or be poured over such an item. These may include charm-stones, fossils, flints, or the metals gold and silver. The potent iron of the magical blacksmith's forge would empower also the water in which items, such as horseshoes, were tempered.[88] Water might also be made holy by bringing it into contact with saintly relics, or by adding scrapings from statues and stone structures associated with the saints. By these methods, we see that water may be considered, in magical practice, to be a conduit of virtue when brought into contact with items and substances of potency. Salt may be added to waters in the rites of clergy and popular magician alike, and water will take on the virtues of any plant substances steeped or boiled within it; boiling being in itself an act with traditional magical associations and applications.

As a conduit, water was traditionally used to 'take on' and transfer ailments within curative folk-magical rites. Conversely however, as previous chapters have attested, water may be possessed of its own innate virtues and potencies, and these may pass into items themselves made 'holy' or potent via their contact with waters of virtue.

Curative Waters

From Michael Howard we learn of a traditional method for making curative charm water, for use on both humans and animals, still employed by an Inverness 'white witch' in the 1970s. Before sunrise, she would drop gold and silver in the form of a wedding ring and an old coin into water, which she had gathered from a burn. This she would then bless by saying over it; "in the name of the trinity, father, son and holy ghost, bless you and may all evil things depart from you".[89]

---

88. Buckland, Raymond. *Gypsy Witchcraft and Magic*, p. 63.
89. Howard, Michael. *Scottish Witches & Warlocks*, p. 147.

In another Scottish method, of the 19th century, a wise-woman would draw the water from a well. Her client would be sat before the hearth, in the presence of fire which might simply be a lighted candle, and the room locked. Into a tablespoon of the well water, the wise-woman would tip a small amount of salt using a borrowed or stolen new silver sixpence. This mixture she would stir with her forefinger, and bless by making the sign of the cross over it in invocation of the Holy Trinity. The feet and hands of the patient would be anointed with this blessed charm water, and a cross marked upon their forehead. The rite was completed by the client retiring to bed to awaken cured of their ailment the next morning.[90]

A coin was employed in the same manner within a Romany method for making curative charm water. Salt is tipped into water, which has been set to boil over a fire, using a found coin. The water is then allowed to cool, whereupon it is flicked onto the hands and feet of the patient, using the coin to do so.[91]

Where plant substances are employed as curatives, water drawn from a spring is sometimes called for; suggesting that the combined virtues of both plant and water are of importance for efficacy. Potent as a protection against evil, The Club Moss – *Lycopodium Inundatum*, was widely regarded for its use in the preparation of fumigations and fomentations for the eyes. In Cornwall, a ritual method for its gathering was recorded by Robert Hunt, 1865:

Go to where the moss grows upon the third day of the moon, when the crescent becomes visible. Show to the moon the knife with which the moss is to be cut, and say; "As Christ healed the issue of blood, do thou cut, what thou cuttest for good!" At

---

90. Ibid.
91. Kemp, Gillian. *The Good Spell Book*, p. 45.

sun-down, and with carefully washed hands, the club-moss is to be cut whilst kneeling. It must then be carefully wrapped in a white cloth, later to be boiled in some water which must be taken from a spring close to its place of growth.

Water, drawn from a well or spring, is also called for in Romany tradition to treat the eyes. Within this water, saffron is to be steeped. When applying the eye water, one must say; "Oh, pain from the eyes go into the water. Go into the water, into the herb. Into the earth. To the Earth Spirit. There is your home; there go and feast."[92]

Alternatively, this eye wash may be made by adding the Saffron to spring water set to boil. It is advised that this should be done on a Sunday, and as well as soothing the eyes and strengthening ordinary sight, it is said also to aid clairvoyant vision.[93]

The special virtue of both the water and the plant substance, combine again in the making of a poultice from Flintshire, Wales. In the bathing pool of the famous St Winefride's Well, grows a moss Jungermannia asplenioides which is known as 'St Winifred's Hair'. Pilgrims would gather and dry this moss, as well as collecting water from the well, using both to prepare a poultice for the cures of sprains and other pains and injuries.[94]

In Cornish magic, bramble leaves and well water were together employed for the charming of burns and inflammations. Nine bramble leaves are immersed in the water of a spring, and three times the following charm is said to each leaf to be passed over the affliction:

---

92. Buckland, Raymond. *Gypsy Witchcraft and Magic*, p. 59.
93. Kemp, Gillian. *The Good Spell Book*, p. 55.
94. Bord, Janet. Cures and Curses – *Ritual and Cult at Holy Wells*, p. 85.

Charm Waters

There came three angels out of the east, one brought fire and two brought frost; out fire and in frost! In the name of the Father, Son, and Holy Ghost. Amen!

In a crossover of Christian and 'pagan' magic, saintly relics would be immersed into water in order to bless and empower it for curative purposes.[95] Small pieces would also be broken off from the statues of saints and ground into a powder to be added to water for the same purposes.

In Clynnog Fwar near Caernarfon, people would make a charm water for the curing of sore eyes by visiting the holy well and nearby chapel of St Beuno; uncle of St Winefride. Water would be drawn from the saint's well, and scrapings taken from the columns within his chapel. The powdered scrapings would be added to the water and applied to the eyes as a curative.[96]

Both holy water and bells have traditionally been believed to possess the power to ward off evil influences. It is perhaps for this reason that Holy water would be poured into and drunk from a bell for healing purposes, thus exorcising the ailment.[97]

Such curative and exorcising influences have also been attributed to certain 'charm stones', the virtues of which were employed via water as a conduit for their power. Such stones could achieve a high level of fame and be kept in hereditary guardianship, and lent out for use in the folk-magical curing of man and beast.

One such stone was employed in this manner in Wales. To cure cattle and sheep, water was poured over the stone, before being given to ailing livestock. To cure people of any malady, physical or mental, the stone

---

95. Ibid, p. 104.
96. Howard, Michael. *Welsh Witches and Wizards*, p. 143, and Bord, Janet & Collin. *Sacred Waters*, p. 214.
97. Bord, Janet. *Cures and Curses – Ritual and Cult at Holy Wells*, p. 13.

would be placed into a bowl of water to be shared out to those who required it. In either use, a charm would be spoken in Welsh over the stone, given here in translation:

O thou stone of might and right, let me dip thee in the water – in the water of pure spring or of wave, in the name of St. David, in the name of the twelve Apostles, in the name of the Holy Trinity, and of Michael and all the angels, in the name of Christ and Mary His mother! Blessings on the clear shining stone! Blessings on the clear pure water! A healing of all bodily ills on man and beast alike!

When the stone was to be lent out, various observances had to be strictly followed by the person fetching it; '[he] must not speak nor sit, nor enter anybody's house, nor be found outside his own house after sunset.'[98]

An example of a charm stone in Ireland, apparently still in use for the treatment of cattle, is the Curraghmore Crystal, today in the possession of the Marquis of Curraghmore. The stone is believed to have been brought to Ireland from the Holy Land in the 12th century. To cure cattle, a running stream was required to act as a conduit for its virtue. In this method, the stone would be held in the flowing waters, just upstream from a ford. Through this, the cattle would be driven, so that the beneficial virtues may be imparted unto them as they entered the stream.[99]

Perhaps the most famous example of a charm stone is the Lee Penny in Scotland, so named for its setting within a 15th century silver groat. It is, like the Curraghmore Crystal, associated with the crusades, and is kept in hereditary guardianship, in this case by the Lockhart Clan. The stone was believed to be possessed of the powers to cure disease in man, horses and cattle.

---

98. Trevelyan, Marie. *Welsh Witchcraft, Charms and Spells*, p. 27.
99. Walker, Charles. *The Encyclopedia of Secret Knowledge*, p. 171-172.

Fitz's Well and Cross, Okehampton.

*Top: clouties tied to tree branches near Cornwall's famous Madron Well.
Above: Madron Well itself.*

*Top: St Cleer Holy Well and Cross, St Cleer, Liskeard.
Above: one of the twin healing wells at Carn Euny, West Cornwall.*

Well-house in the garden of Castle Horneck Lodge, the site of a reputed eye-healing well.

The Norman font of St Martin's Church, Lewannick, Cornwall, carved with labyrinths, spirals and pentagrams.

Cecil Williamson's 'moon rake' (top) and mirror-bottomed copper basin, used within magical operations employing a pond, the light of the full moon and the client's urine. Museum of Witchcraft & Magic, Boscastle.

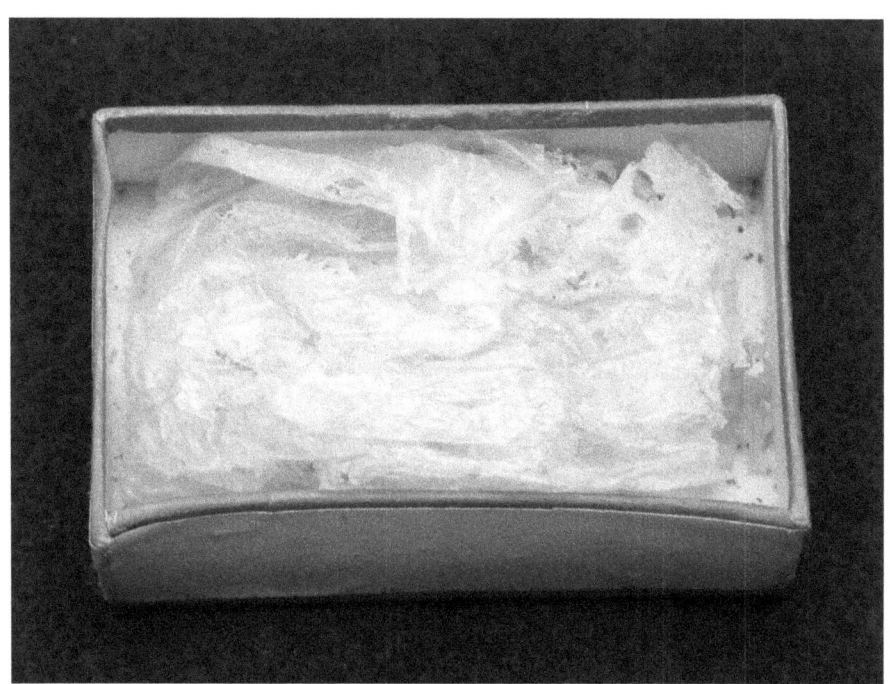

A child's caul (top), a sought-after amulet against drowning at sea.

the heart of a seagull (above) stuck with pins, used in South Devon against malefic magic. Both from Scarborough Museum's Clarke collection of charms and amulets.

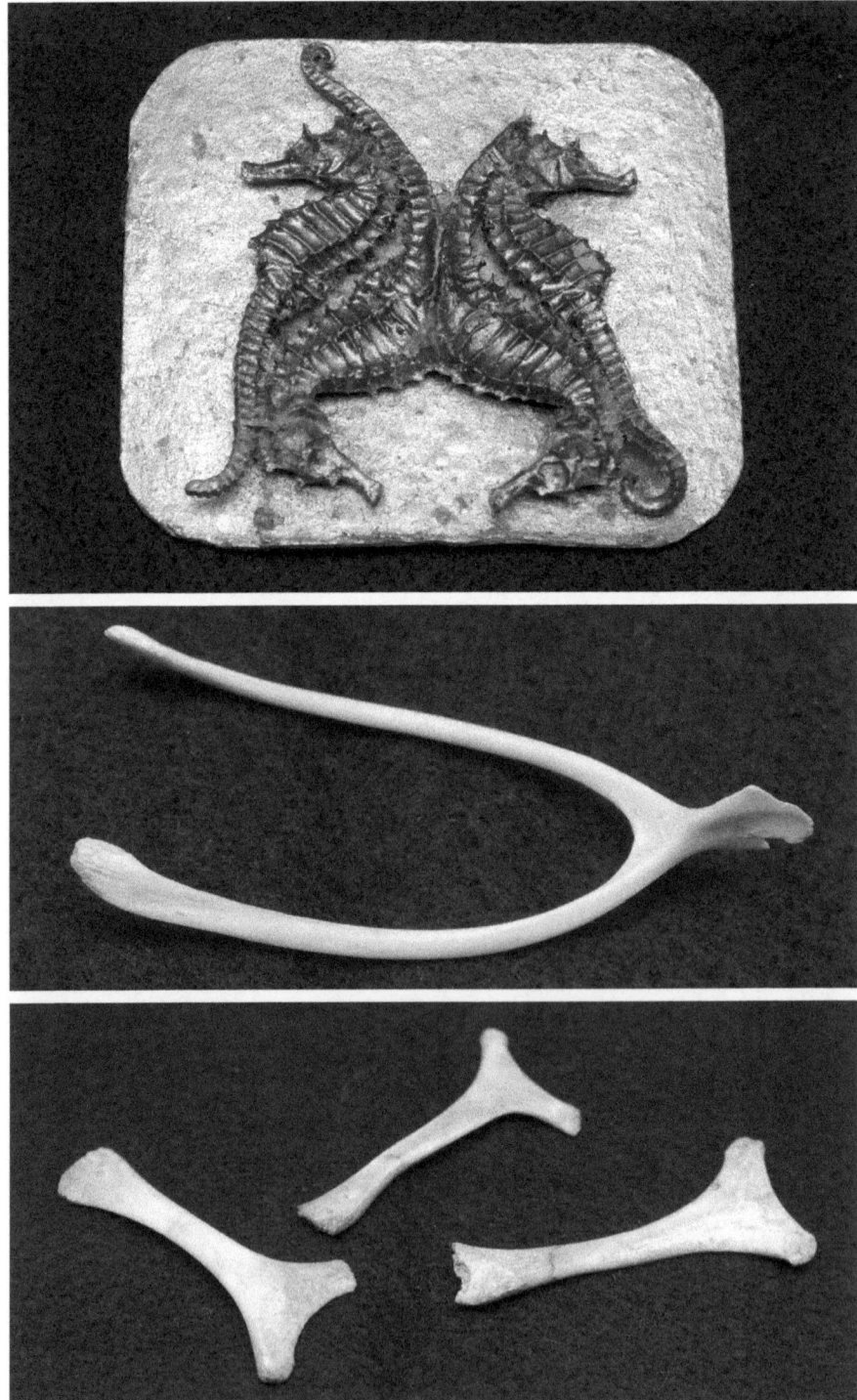

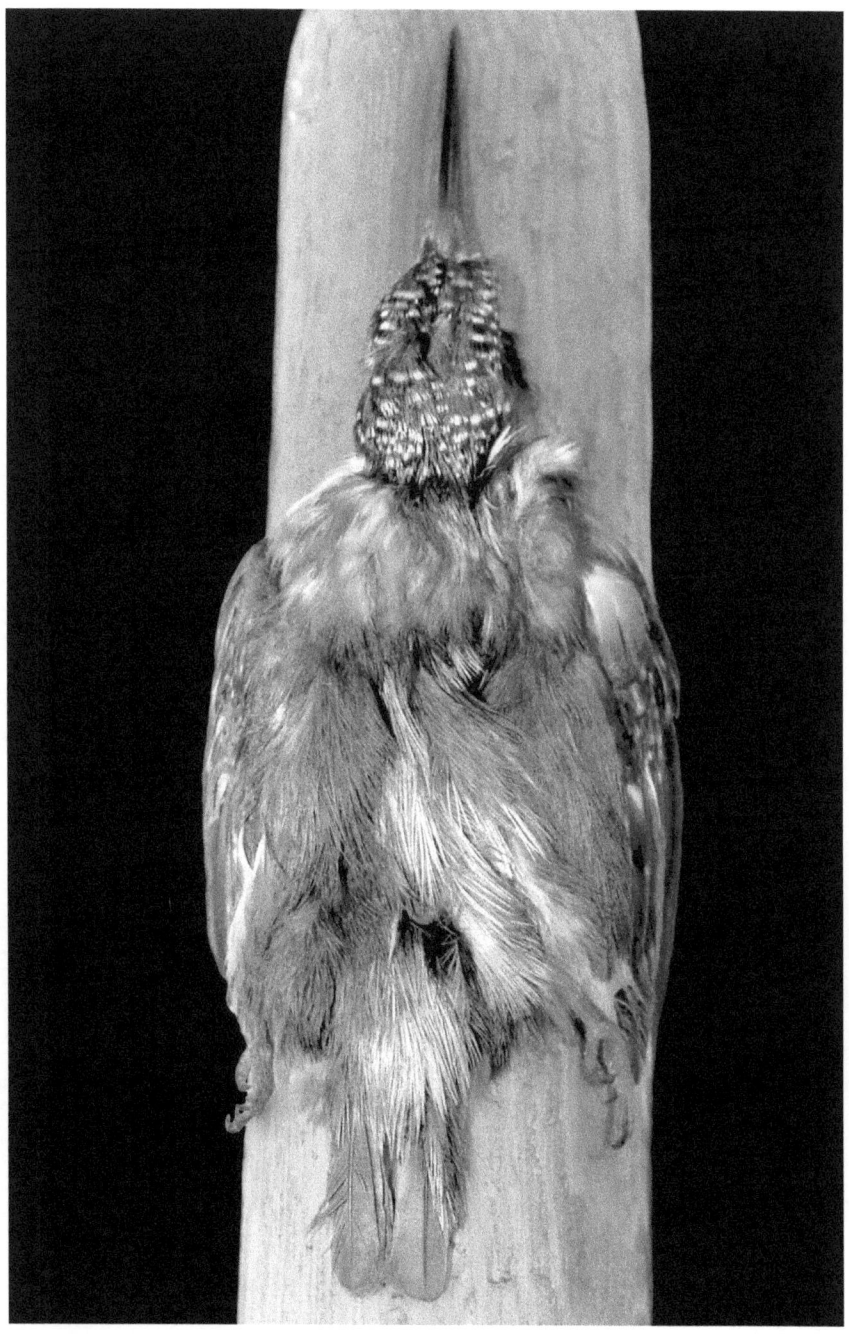

Facing: a seahorse amulet against the evil eye. A fowl's wishbone, called a 'merrythought' and carried by South Devon sailors. Sheep hyoid bones, carried as charms by Scarborough fishermen. Above: A Kingfisher skin, complete with beak, nailed to the mast of a Guernsey fishing vessel in an act of sympathetic magic. All from Scarborough Museum's Clarke collection of charms and amulets.

The sea witchcraft cabinet in Steve Patterson's Gwithti an Pystri – A Cabinet of Folklore & Magic, Famouth, Cornwall.

Facing: the 'Zennor Mermaid' bench-end in the church of St Senara, in the hamlet of Zennor, West Cornwall

Molybdomancy (top) and oomancy (above) – the divinatory arts of pouring molten mteals (usually lead) and egg-white, respectively, into water in order to read the resulting forms and shapes for meaning. Stills from the short film 'Divination'.

Charm Waters

The stone was employed in a number of ways, all of which required a vessel of water. It might be dipped thrice and then swirled round once in the water. It might instead be drawn around the vessel, and then thrice dipped. The water was then either drunk, or used to bathe the patient's affliction. To cure cattle, in the early 18th century, it is recorded that the amulet would be inserted into the cloven end of a stick and immersed in a tub of water from which the cattle would then drink. In all cases, no words were to be spoken during the stone's use, or the efficacy of the procedure would be destroyed.

Presumably in order to be kept for use when required, and to act as a charm to ward of illness, phials of water in which the Lee Penny had been immersed were hung within cattle byres.[1]

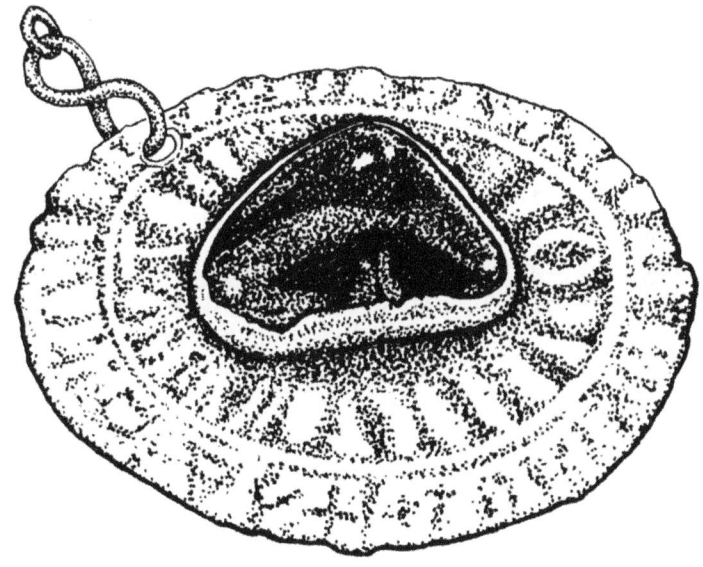

Payment for the stone's use would not necessarily be required by its keepers, but a deposit often was. During

---
1. Bord, Janet & Collin. *Sacred Waters*, p. 69.

the reign of Charles I, it is said that the people of Newcastle had been loaned the charm stone during an outbreak of plague. The town gave a bond of £6000 to guarantee its safe return. Such was their faith in the potency of the amulet that the town requested to forfeit the bond so that the people of Newcastle could retain the stone; this offer was however declined.

The Lee Penny was in popular use throughout times in which extreme penalties existed in Scotland for those engaging in acts that could be considered allied to witchcraft. In the late 17th century, the amulet's keeper; Sir James Lockhart of the Lee, was formally accused of employing a charm for curative purposes. However, as no words were spoken during the stone's use, he was found not guilty of witchcraft, a practice which, it was claimed, required uttered charms and incantations, and that simply inserting a stone into water was not witchcraft and therefore perfectly legal.

Ammonite fossils were also employed as charm stones to cure cattle in 17th century Scotland. They were known as 'cramp stones' because cattle afflicted with cramp would be treated by being bathed in water in which a 'cramp stone' had been steeped for a number of hours.[2]

Another type of charm stone might be both blamed for injuring cattle, and employed in their treatment. Elf-shooting, the belief in which extended from the Shetland Islands to Cornwall,[3] was the practice whereby an elf might inflict injury, even death by firing an elf-stone at their victim. These elf-stones themselves, which tend to be prehistoric flint arrowheads, interestingly are said to have watery origins, for one tradition states that the elves inherited these stones from the elder fairies who wore

---

2. The Museum of Witchcraft and Magic.

3. Henderson, William. *Witchcraft, Toadlore and Charms of the Northern Counties*, p. 7.

the stones as breastpins. The fairies however, are said to have inherited the stones from the mermaids.[4]

In an Irish account of elf-shooting, a charmer, or cunning-man, was brought in to remedy the situation. Finding one of his cows lying down, and in obvious pain, a farmer suspected that she had suffered an elf-shot, and so he went off, seeking the aid of the 'old man' of the county, who was skilled in the curing of cattle. When he arrived, on foot, he cleared the room and prepared a new and clean pot of water to which he added a crooked sixpence and a pound of gunpowder, and set the whole thing to boil. Allowing the mixture to cool, he carried it out to the ailing cow awaiting in the byre, and there set it down before her to drink. It is said the gunpowder immediately blew the elf-stone out through the wound, and that the sixpence covered the whole made upon the cow's heart, restoring her to health.[5]

In treatment, cattle might be given water to drink in which an elf-stone had been immersed. In Scarborough Museum there is a Neolithic flint arrowhead which was employed in Antrim to cure cattle of 'grup', by giving them water in which the arrowhead had been boiled.

A good Scottish example of water's use as a conduit for curative purposes also features the magic of liminality, spring water, and 'passing-on-magic'. A man in the late 18th century, suffering severe rheumatic pain, called upon the assistance of a 'white witch'. The man was instructed to draw water from a spring, and to take it to a stile in an ancient hedge at sunrise. Meeting him there, the witch used the water to bathe her client's limbs whilst speaking Psalm 23. By this act, the man's pain had been charmed away, but the rite was not yet complete, for he had to pour the remainder of the spring water

---

4. Ibid, p. 6.
5. Henderson, William. *Witchcraft, Toadlore and Charms of the Northern Counties*, p. 8.

over the old stile, into which, the witch explained, the affliction would be transferred and passed on to the next person to cross it.[6]

In Welsh charming, a method was employed by which water would act as a conduit for the removal of a headache. Before the patient, the charmer would have prepared two bowls, one filled with cold water, and the other filed with molten tallow. A carding comb was also required. Three times the head of the patient would be held within the cold water for a few seconds, as the molten tallow was poured through the carding comb into the water. When this procedure was complete, the water and tallow were separated and disposed of; the water had to be poured onto the nearest elder tree, and the tallow thrown upon the fire whereupon the headache would be cured.[7]

Retaliative Magic & Counter Charming

The boiling of water, perhaps with plant materials, was employed within folk magic both to punish wrongdoers, and to counter evil. It is said that boiled water is loathed by the Devil, and a taboo existed against taking boiled water into the bedroom, for such an act would cause offence to the Devil, who would thereafter cause trouble within the household.[8] Why the bedroom should be set aside, however, as a place where care should be taken not to offend the Devil is not explained.

A 'boiling' rite, employing both magic and a strong psychological component, to punish a man who had been mistreating his wife and children was witnessed

---

6. Howard, Michael. *Scottish Witches & Warlocks*, p. 114.
7. Trevelyan, Marie. *Welsh Witchcraft, Charms and Spells*, p. 20-21.
8. Pickering, David. *Dictionary of Witchcraft*, p. 278.

by Cecil Williamson. A number of people associated with the situation are invited to attend the rite which, in the modern day, would take place in the kitchen. When all are assembled, the edges of the doors, widows, and any other openings to the room are closed and sealed with tape. A large iron pot is placed upon the hob, filled with water, and various herbs and plants added. Cecil witnessed the use of groundsel, dandelion, verbena and cabbage. As the contents of the pot begin to boil, a tightly corked bottle of the victim's urine is put in, and all wait, uncomfortably in the sealed steam-filled hot room, until, eventually, the bottle of urine explodes.

A few days after the rite has been performed, its victim will begin to suffer stomach pains. Here, a character called a 'white witch' or the 'runner' comes into play. She will call upon the victim to hear of his affliction, and persuade him that it is the result of ill-wishing, for he must be doing something that is upsetting someone. Thus, he is persuaded to think upon his behaviour and change his ways.

Devonshire witch-lore tells of a white witch brought in to reverse the ill-fortunes of a farming family, brought about by maleficia. Boiling appears to have been employed as one part of his lengthy and complex magical operations against the wrongdoer. The family had offended a thoroughly unpleasant 'black witch' known as Old Hannah, and had been devastated by a long series of misfortunes. To begin his work in remedying the situation, the white witch from Chard, came to live on the farm. Throughout his operations, he kept a great cauldron of water boiling over a fire with barley added to it, which was for the protection of the horses. Over the fire, six bullocks' hearts were hung, two of which were stuck full with needles and pins, and the other four with maiden nails. For his work, which took a month to complete, and resulted in the death of Old Hannah and the full recovery of the farm, the white witch received a payment of £100.[9]

A Flemish counter charm against ill-wishing involves the use of water to form a likeness of the evildoer. A vessel of water is prepared before the client, and lead melted over a fire. This is then to be poured into the water whereupon the lead shall solidify in anthropomorphic form. The evil that the client has suffered by bewitchment is then to be returned to the evildoer. The operator will ask their client to choose where upon the body of their aggressor the evil is to be returned, and, once the part has been chosen, the operator will make a cut upon that part of the leaden image.[10]

Protections & Warding

In addition to waters being drawn from certain wells at certain times of the year to be bottled and brought home as a protective charm, or the waters of the Lee Penny, hung up to ward the cattle byres, that charm waters may be prepared specifically for the purpose of sprinkling over people, animals, items and places, or to anoint the places of liminality within the home (the doors, windows and hearth) is well known.

Employed within the warding rites of the Church and folk-magic alike, and being found within the circle rites of some streams of contemporary witchcraft, salt and water may most commonly and simply be combined for the purposes of protective sprinkling and anointing.

In the magic of the Grimoire, and the Bible, we find the use of water as a conduit for the exorcising and purifying virtues of herbs within ritual acts of asperging.

---

9. Farquharson-Coe, A. *Devon's Witchcraft*, p. 27-29.

10. Henderson, William. *Witchcraft, Toadlore and Charms of the Northern Counties*, p. 51.

Charm Waters

As we have seen, the immersing of gold and silver was employed within Scotland to form a charm water for the exorcism of illness. In the Northwest of Scotland, these precious metals were employed to prepare a charm water to exorcise the influence of the evil eye from 'overlooked children'. The 'gold and silver water' was made by dropping a shilling and a sovereign into water, which is then to be sprinkled over the child in the name of the Holy Trinity.[11]

As well as receiving virtue from items and materials immersed within it, sacred waters had the power to give virtue unto items, thus making them charms. We find this occurrence at St Olcan's Holy Well, Cranfield, Antrim. Here, amber coloured stones of gypsum, known as 'Cranfield Pebbles', were highly sought after as charm stones. By carrying one of these stones, it was believed that one would be protected from drowning, thus they were in demand by fishermen who carried them aboard their boats, and that the home in which they were kept would be safe from fire and burglary. It was also believed that by keeping a Cranfield Pebble close during childbirth protection would be afforded to both mother and child in what was often a dangerous process.[12]

The popular use of holy water, brought from church, is found in the tradition that those who bathed their eyes with water used within the rite of baptism would be protected from seeing a ghost.[13] Holy water used in Easter church services, was believed to be invested with extra potency in the warding off of witches and evil spirits, whilst holy water employed at Palm Sunday was kept to as a preventative against storms.

---

11. Ibid, p. 9.

12. antrimtown.co.uk & Bord, Janet & Colin. *Sacred Waters*, p. 105.

13. Bord, Janet. Cures and Curses – *Ritual and Cult at Holy Wells*, p. 10.

Divinations

Holy water it seemed was also possessed of the ability to reveal the identity of witches who had shape-shifted into bestial form. To discover if a cat was really a witch employing such a disguise, it would be placed within a bowl that had previously been used to hold holy water. If the cat attempted to escape from the bowl, its identity as a witch was revealed. Given the likelihood of any cat being compliant with such a procedure, it must have been found that nearly all cats were in fact witches.

As we have seen with holy wells and sacred springs, water may be seen to be possessed of the virtue, or an indwelling spirit, able to influence the movement of items placed upon its surface in acts of divination.

Water employed within such rites need not necessarily be that of a sacred or numinous locus, for, in Welsh tradition, water from any source may be placed within a pan for the purpose. In marital divinations, to lengths of straw, or sticks, may be set to float upon the surface of the water, after having first been named after those they represent. If they should float towards each other, then a marriage is foretold, but if one shall float away from the other, then the relationship is doomed to fail; the fault resting with the one that floats away.

The same rite would be performed to divine which of a married couple would be the first to die. This would be indicated by the first of the two straws or sticks to sink beneath the surface.[14]

Matrimonial divinations in Suffolk might employ the prophetic virtues contained within the first egg to be laid by a hen, revealed by the agency of water. The maid who wishes to discover the trade of her future husband should break the egg into a clear vessel of water, there

---

14. Trevelyan, Marie. *Welsh Witchcraft, Charms and Spells*, p. 32.

to be left over night. By the morning, the white of the egg will have taken on forms which will be in some way suggestive of a trade or profession. If, for example, the shape of a shoe or boot can be discerned, then the one the diviner is to marry will be a shoemaker, if scissors are revealed, a tailor he will be etc.[15]

---

15. Gurdon, Eveline Camilla (Ed.). *Old Suffolk Love and Cure Charms*, p. 26.

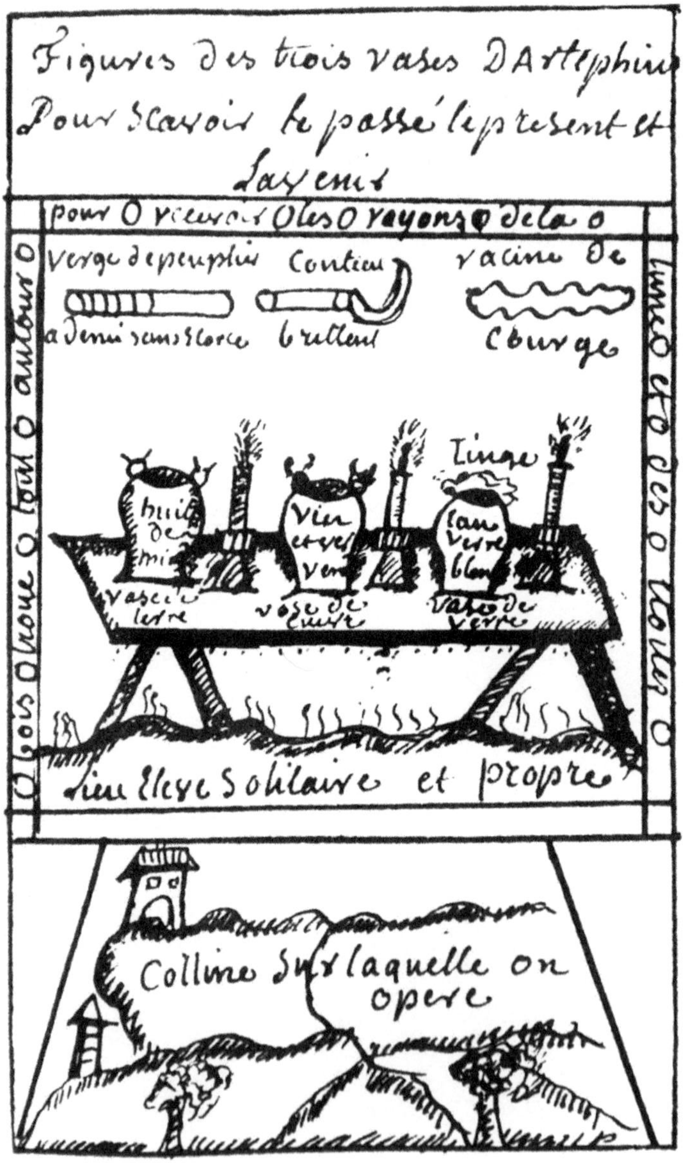
Figures des trois vases DArtephius
Pour scavoir le passé le present et
Lavenir
pour O recevoir O les O rayons O dela O
O bois O roue O tout O autour O
lune O et O des O etoiles O
verge de peuplier
a demi sans escorce
Couteau
brullant
racine de
Courge
Tinge
Vase de terre
vase de cuivre
Vase de verre
lieu Eleve solitaire et propre
Colline sur laquelle on opere

Methods of Hydromancy

Hydromancy, the practice of making oracular and divinatory use of water, is a collective term for a variety of specific methods and rites. Within our exploration of the popular magic of holy wells, we have found a variety of means to conjure prophecy, via the arising of bubbles, the changing clarity of the water, the floating or sinking of objects placed into the water or the movements they made whilst doing so, the formation of visions, and the movements of eels or fish inhabiting the waters. In the magic of pools we find the floating of bread to discover the location of a drowned body, and in the magic of streams and rivers were children employed to indicate the direction of stolen horses, and divinations made by the changing colours of the Thames, or from visions or the number of ripples arising there from. Also we have seen the ability of water to model prophetic forms from substances poured within it.

The employment of water to conjure forth prophetic visions, to manifest which, depending upon opinion, occurs within the water itself or within the 'mind's eye' of the practitioner, in acts of 'scrying' is perhaps the most familiar form of hydromancy to the contemporary witch and occultist. It is however a method of established pedigree, with a number of traditional variations.

The conjuration of images, for divinatory purposes, onto the surface of water contained within a magical vessel is properly termed castronomancy. Whilst some practitioners have preferred to employ clear water, perhaps with a silver coin lying at its bottom to provide a point of focus, others have found it helpful to blacken their scrying water with substances such as India Ink. The employment of water drawn from a spring for the purposes of conjuring divinatory images is given its own term; pegomancy. The tumultuous and seething surface of water, set to boil in a vessel over fire, also presents a captivating medium for the seeking of both visions and sounds of prophecy.[16]

A famed and complex operation of scrying, attributed to Artephius and known as 'The Vases of Artephius', combines a form of hydromantic castronomancy via the use of water, oinomancy via the use of wine, and eleomancy via the use of an oil.

The operation is to be performed in a solitary and high place, far from interruptions and noise, where a table is set up upon two trestles. This is to be surrounded by some wooden enclosure, pierced all over with holes, so as to admit rays of light from the sun, moon or stars. More precise details of this structure and its nature are lacking.

Silence is to be strictly observed throughout all operations at the site, and all the instruments are to be shielded from the sun. Upon beginning the operation, the weather must be very calm and clear, and must have been so for the three preceding days. The clarity of the skies shall allow the daytime operations to be under the full light of the sun, and by night under the full light of the moon and stars.

The operator of this work is to be robed in white, and with a full head covering of red silk or linen, leaving

---

16. Walker, Charles. *The Encyclopedia of Secret Knowledge*, p. 190-191.

Methods of Hydromancy

only the eyes unconcealed. Required also are a wand of poplar wood, one half of which is striped of its bark, a knife, and a pumpkin root. Their function and manner of employment within the rite are not given.

Upon the enclosed table, three vessels are to be arranged; to the left a vessel containing oil of myrrh, in the centre a vessel containing wine, and to the right a vessel containing water. The oil vessel is to be of earthenware, the wine vessel of green earthenware or of copper, and the water vessel of white earthenware or of glass. It is mentioned that a cloth is placed upon the vessel of water, and that each vessel has placed beside it a candle.

Within the vessel of oil, the diviner may perceive a vision of the appearance of the person involved, or the past of the situation, in the wine may be revealed the thing or event itself and the present, and in the water a 'shadow' of the thing or event and the future.[17]

Via lecanomancy may divinations be made by observing the behaviours presented within water held within a dish or basin when objects or substances have been placed within it. Stones were commonly thrown into the water to cause ripples and sounds which may be interpreted by the lecanomancer. Precious stones might be employed for this purpose,[18] sometimes three in number, but ordinary rocks and stones seem also to be acceptable. Instead of stones, flower or oil might be added to the water, and their movements and formations upon the surface interpreted.

Within the magic of holy wells, we have encountered a form of prophetic augury via the observance of the movements of fish or eels inhabiting the well. This divinatory practice of ichthyomancy was performed anciently by casting pieces of meat into water, and

---

17. Ibid. & de Givry, Grillot. *Witchcraft: Magic and Alchemy*, p. 308.
18. Walker, Charles. *The Encyclopedia of Secret Knowledge*, p. 190.

making readings from the reactions and movements of fish dwelling therein.[19]

We have also encountered the popular divinatory practice of making readings from the contents of eggs added to water – oomancy. As in the example encountered, the white of the egg is added to cold water, and left for a number of hours for the divinatory forms to occur. Sometimes salt would be added to the water in this method.[20] Far more immediate however, is the method of dropping the separated egg-white into boiling water.

Within the practice of ceromancy, molten wax is employed to mediate prophecy within the forms it assumes when dropped into water. In some practices, boiling water is used, and the waxen formations read when the water has cooled,[21] however, cold water will of course produce instant forms ready for interpretation.

Molybdomancy, is essentially the same divinatory practice, but instead employing molten metals. Often lead is employed for its low melting point, and possibly its Saturnian virtue, in which case the practice is more properly called plumbomancy. Again, either boiling water or cold water may be employed within the method. Within Nordic countries, it remains a popular practice within the traditions of New Year celebrations. The forms studied for divinatory meaning may be those assumed by the lead itself, or by the shadows cast by it against candlelight. According to Cecil Williamson, it was a practice popular amongst witches in the South-West to make divinations by melting lead over a fire and then allowing it to drip

---

19. Ibid, p. 199.
20. Ibid, p. 201.
21. Ibid, p. 191.

Methods of Hydromancy

from a height into their water-filled cauldrons and copper preserving pans.[22]

Aleuromancy, the divinatory practice of obtaining readings from flour or grains may employ water. A bowl filled with water, may have flour added to it. The diviner, taking the bowl in their hands, will swirl and swill away the water, leaving formations and patterns of wet flour within the bowl which are interpreted for divinatory meaning.[23] The practice, already encountered of floating a loaf of bread upon water to locate a drowned body is, strictly speaking, another form of aleuromancy for it includes the use of baked flours and grains.

---

22. The Museum of Witchcraft and Magic.
23. Walker, Charles. *The Encyclopedia of Secret Knowledge*, p. 201.

Beings, Spirits & Deities of the Dark Waters

The Otherworldly atmosphere which haunts the waters of the earth; windows into another reality, is entirely fitting to the various spirit folk, long held by traditional lore to inhabit such places, and with whom, at the water's edge, humans may engage and interact via various means. The sea has always been to us, and remains so, a veil unto a hidden and unknown world, home to unimaginable creatures. Even in our present age, the light of scientific illumination is yet to reveal more than brief tentative glimpses of a minute proportion of the darkest depths and fathomless abysses where mystery remains. Much of the life of the deep oceans that has been recorded, classified and catalogued would not look at all out of place within an ancient fantastical bestiary, and so it is understandable that humanity has long seen the unknowable seas, the vast lakes and the dark pools of the land to be inhabited by supernatural beings; part corporeal, part spirit, and often of probable Divine, or semi-Divine origin. The legendary water serpents and dragons, of which the Loch Ness Monster is a famed and persistent example, dwelling in the seas, lakes, rivers, pools and wells, are again spirit-creatures of liminality. As ancient emblems and vehicles of primordial Divine and chthonic force, the serpent of the waters is illustrative of water's role as intermediary and a window unto the Otherworldly.

Of the seas, but also of lakes and rivers, the Mermaid is a better known example of a being, liminal in nature; occupying a state somewhere between the physical and the spiritual, and who may pass between the waters and land. In Cornwall; a peninsula of land surrounded by ocean and whose coasts are peppered with small and ancient harbour villages where livings were made via the sea, it is of little surprise that a rich corpus of merfolk-lore exists; merged in some cases with folk-magical tradition and witchcraft.

Numerous tales were told of the 'merry-maids', occasionally leaving their watery abodes to walk upon the land, being possessed of the ability to transform their physicality, via which amorous encounters with mortal man may occur. Often the man returns to the sea with the merry-maid, never to be seen again; perhaps the remnant echo of ancient goddess beliefs and themes of sacrifice. Some, however, would from such encounters be invested with magical abilities, which would forever be passed along the bloodline. Such stories of encounters between mankind and supernatural beings as 'pellar foundation myths' are intriguingly reminiscent of traditions within the Old Craft of ancient unions between man and the gods or the faery, fallen angels or the Watchers, resulting in the skills of magic being given unto man and the establishment of a magical bloodline within the human race. Intriguingly, it is suggested that, in Romany tradition, a witch may be created via carnal union between a woman and a spirit of the waters.[24]

The theme may be discerned within the Cornish story of 'The old Man of Cury' or 'Lutey and the Mermaid'. The tale tells of an elderly man, from the parish of Cury, walking one of the coves of the Lizard Peninsular

---

24. Buckland, Raymond. *Gypsy Witchcraft and Magic*, p. 33.

in a meditative state – perhaps suggesting a shift in consciousness whereby he found himself 'between the worlds.' Within the cove old Lutey encountered a beautiful mermaid; she was in a state of distress as she had become stranded by the ebbing tide. She begged the old man to carry her back to the sea, and that in return he would have whatever three things he wished for. So he lifted her upon his back and conveyed her towards the waters whilst speaking of his wishes. The first was the power to break the spells of witchcraft, the second was the power to charm away diseases, and third was the power to discover thieves, and restore stolen goods.

Each of these powers she promised the old man would be his, but he would have to meet her upon a certain day at a half-tide rock, where she would instruct him in the abilities he wished for. Upon reaching the water, the mermaid drew a comb out of her hair and gave it to the old man with the instruction that he may use it to call upon her by combing the waters.

Upon the arrival of the appointed day, the old man met with the mermaid at the half-tide rock, and was there instructed in the ways and mysteries of the pellar. From that day he became skilled in such ways as lifting the ill-influence of witchcraft from man and beast, to prepare a vessel of water in which to conjure the image of thieves, to charm shingles, tetters, St Antony's fire, and St Vitus's dance as well as knowing 'all the mysteries of bramble leaves and the like'. It was long said that these magical abilities were passed down his bloodline through generations of pellar.

Possible thematic links with goddess tradition and the Otherworld might be perceived within this story in versions where the mermaid unsuccessfully requests that the old man return with her beneath the waves to her world, where he would be restored to youth and remain ever young. Suggestive also of the Underworld and the realm of the dead is the description of her home:

'Come with me, love, and see the beauty of the mermaid's dwellings. Yet the ornaments, with which we take the most delight to embellish our halls and chambers, are the noble sons and fair daughters of earth, whom the wind and waves send in foundered ships to our abodes. Come, I will show you thousands of handsome bodies so embalmed, in a way only known to ourselves, with choice salts and rare spices, that they look more beautiful than when they breathed... Aye, and when you see their limbs all adorned with glistening gems, move gracefully to and fro with the motion of the waves, you will think they still live.[25]

Sacrifice, and a theme reminiscent of the Devil's toll; the payment of one's life following the attainment of magical powers by diabolic compact, may also be discerned within the tale. Exactly nine years following his compact with the mermaid, a number heavily associated with the moon and goddess tradition, Lutey is lost whilst fishing in his boat on perfectly calm waters under the light of the moon. At midnight, the waters about the boat erupted into a tumultuous foam from which the mermaid appeared. "My hour is come" said Lutey, before he jumped from his boat to swim to the mermaid and was never seen again, and it was said that every nine years thereafter, at least one of his descendants would be claimed by the sea.

Often to be seen held by mermaids in their depictions is the mirror and the comb. It has been suggested that the mirror may be symbolic of the moon, or the apple; associated with wisdom and the Otherworld, whilst the comb could have originally been a depiction of a stringed instrument by which the 'sea-siren' may entice mortal men.[26]

---

25. Bottrell, William. *Traditions and Hearthside Stories of West Cornwall.*
26. Cooke, Ian. *Mermaid to Merrymaid – Journey to the Stones,* p. 39.

Perhaps Cornwall's most famous mermaid legend is that associated with Zennor, and clearly illustrates the 'merry-maid' as a liminal and supernatural being. The story tells of a mermaid who would periodically leave the sea to walk upon land in human form and attend services in Zennor Church, where today visitors may see the famous bench-end carved do depict the mermaid. Her beauty and skills in singing were beyond those of mortal women, and she was always richly attired in the finest of gowns. Now matter how long a period of time had passed between her visits, she never aged and she remained a mystery; marvelled at in wonder by the people of Zennor. Upon one of her visits, a young man, and the best singer in the parish named Mathey Trewella caught her eye. He followed her from church, and neither he, nor the mysterious woman, was seen again. Upon sightings of a mermaid in a nearby cove, it was concluded that this was the true identity of their enigmatic visitor, and that young Mathey Trewella had been enchanted away to her world.

As seems generally to be the case with Otherworldly beings, the causing of offence is likely to result in serious repercussions. Legend tells that the small Cornish fishing town of Padstow was home to a deep natural harbour, able to receive the largest of vessels and home to a guardian merry-maid. Arising to the surface one day, a fool with a gun took a shot at her, causing her to retreat quickly beneath the surface, however, she arose again, raised her right hand and uttered a curse upon the harbour. From that day forth it became choked with relentless drifting sands rendering it almost useless.

A similar tale is told of a sand-beach near Looe called Seaton. It is said that it was once home to a thriving town, but became consumed by sand following a curse placed by a mermaid who had suffered some injury from one of the lost town's sailors.

Cornwall's merry-maids were quite capable of acting in a manner of benefit to humankind. To the west of Lamorna's beautiful cove is to be found a rock known as 'The Mermaid's Rock', and here, it was said, a mermaid would appear to forewarn the people of coming storms with her beautiful, yet sombre singing to which the spirits of those lost at sea would join in with mournful cries, echoing about the sea-cliffs. However, young men were said to have walked into the sea to swim off to the rock upon hearing her song, never to return, and so the darker sacrificial themes of the merry-maid continue.

In Scottish and Welsh tradition, another liminal and supernatural woman of part bestial form, possessed of shape shifting abilities and associated with water, is the Glaistig. When seen, she is tall, thin, grey of skin and dressed in the faery colour of green. Her hood conceals long yellow hair, and beneath her gown are hidden her goat-like legs and cloven hooves, yet she could assume a form fully human or bestial as she wished. Her Gaelic name means water imp,[27] and her haunts are the lochs, rivers, pools, wells and waterfalls. Associated with cattle, and their guardianship, and the plentiful production of milk, offerings of the first milk of the day were made to her upon special stones, failure to do so would result in the milk herd becoming dry.

Within the folklore of the Isle of Man is another being, similar in name, a shape shifter, and a spirit of the waters. The Glastyn is a supernatural 'water horse' who could assume the form of a beautiful young man. In this form he would attract young women when they were alone, and take them out to sea to their deaths; a theme reminiscent of those encountered within the legends of the merry-maids.

The theme continues within the legends of another water horse; the Kelpie. Said to take the form of a great

---

27. Howard, Michael. *Scottish Witches & Warlocks*, p. 166.

Beings, Spirits & Deities of the Dark Waters

black horse, always dripping with water, the Kelpie haunts the rivers and lochs where it lures humans to feed upon. The Kelpie is possessed of the ability to assume either male or female form in order to attract women or men to their deaths. In equine form however, the Kelpie would take those who mistook it for a mortal horse, and mounted its back, straight into the waters to devour them.

If, however, a person managed to remove a Kelpie's bridle, they were in possession of a powerful charm which imparted upon them the abilities of foresight. By looking through the bridle, such people could also observe the world of faery, the inhabitants of which would be at their bidding; another folkloric exemplar of powers imparted unto humans via interaction with Otherworldly beings.[28]

The old traditions of faery unions, the passing of Otherworldly gnosis and abilities unto human kind and the creation of faery-human hybrid offspring is illustrated potently within the Welsh legends of the Physicians of Myddfai. This hereditary line of healers, skilled in all manner of cures and herbal remedies, and of whom physicians, doctors and surgeons have been known to claim descent until at least the 19th century, is said to have begun by the union in marriage of an ancestor, a herdsman, with a faery woman from a lake called Llyn y Fon Fach in the Black Mountains in the 12th century.

Upon the herdsman's falling in love with the 'lady of the lake', marriage was agreed to with the condition that it would end when the herdsman had struck the faery woman three times. The faery folk of the lake it seems were not above a little trickery, and their definition of being 'struck' appears to have been unfairly broad and included the man gently touching

---

28. Ibid, p. 169-170.

his faery bride's arm to comfort her when she was crying. The marriage inevitably ended following the third 'strike', but not before the union had produced three sons. The faery woman returned to the depths of the lake, followed by her large dowry of fine faery cattle. However, the lady of the lake later resurfaced to teach her half human sons the faery arts of healing and herbalism, and so began the line of the legendary Myddfai Physicians.[29]

Whilst the spirits of the waters' Underworld realms may often present themselves in folklore and tradition with fair and alluring youthful beauty, some who haunt the lakes, pools and rivers are more overtly representative of the dark and primal creatrix/destroyer/fate goddess of the Underworld.

The Cailleach of Scottish, Irish and Manx tradition is one such manifestation of the 'old hag' spirit, possessed of the ability to create hills, mountains and lakes, to cause storms, usher in the winter and foretell death.

In Moray, people in the 19th century believed that the Cailleach lived within a stone cairn at the end of Lochan na Cailliche. As well as haunting the loch, she was believed by the people to be causing illness and bringing death to man and beast. Clergy had attempted unsuccessfully exorcise her, however, the people apparently believed her to take the form of a heron, for when one was shot by an ex-soldier using a gun loaded with silver, she was thought no longer to haunt the loch.[30]

The belief that the Cailleach haunted river fords, where she would await to drown passing travellers[31] is exemplary of the connection between the Cailleach and the bean-nighe, or the 'washer at the ford'. This figure

---

29. Lewis, Gareth. *The Faery Doctors*, The Cauldron No. 103.
30. Bord, Janet & Colin. *Sacred Waters*, p. 148-149.
31. *Ibid.*

wears the faery colour of green and is part bestial in form for she has the webbed feet of a goose.[32]

The 'washer at the ford' would foretell death by her nocturnal apparition at fords, lochs, burns and river-pools washing the bloody clothes or death shrouds of those soon to die.[33] Her role at the liminal ford as harbinger of death in mankind reveals her to be a manifestation of the dark goddess of fate.[34]

---

32. Howard, Michael. *Scottish Witches & Warlocks*, p. 26.
33. Bord, Janet & Colin. *Sacred Waters*, p. 159.
34. *Ibid*, p. 14, & Howard, Michael. *Scottish Witches & Warlocks*, p. 26.

However, as with other such spirits and beings, powers and wisdom may yet be gained by humankind via encounters with the bean-nighe. Any who were brave and skilled enough to approach the bean-nighe by stealth, could win immunity from her powers, have her answer truthfully any questions put to her about the future and claim her as their 'foster mother'. To achieve this, after approaching her spectre unseen, they had to take one of her empty pendulous breasts in their mouth.[35]

Another of her manifestations in Welsh folklore is the Gwrach y Rhibyn; an ugly and pale hag figure, with withered limbs, wild hair, long black teeth and talons. Again she is part bestial in form; possessing large leathery wings like those of a bat and able to fly. She is associated with places of liminality; crossroads and streams, and is said to have haunted the Caerphilly swamp, Glamorgan, which became a lake in wet weather.[36] The Gwrach y Rhibyn too was a foreteller of impending death, for she would approach the window of one about to die, calling their name, or would walk invisibly beside those soon to die, crying, groaning and wailing mournfully.

Whilst water deities of a darker nature, associated with death and the Underworld, may have become feared 'spirits' of folklore and tradition; their original Divine status is either debated or regarded as highly probable, a number of water deities associated with healing traditions within the British Isles are of undoubted origin or status.

Arguably most famous is the healing cult of Sulis Minerva at Bath, where the existing cult of the ancient British healing goddess Sulis was merged with that of the Roman goddess Minerva. Although the sacred springs of Sulis Minerva were a heavily visited centre for magical healing rites, via bathing and the making of offerings unto the waters, sometimes of votive representations of

---

35. *Ibid.*
36. Bord, Janet & Colin. *Sacred Waters*, p. 159.

the body parts to be cured, it was also a locus for curse magic where lead defixiones were also left.[37]

The Romans also embraced the British deity Nodens, and built a healing centre dedicated to him within an Iron Age hill-fort at Lydney Park, overlooking the Severn Estuary. The healing complex included baths, and incubatory facilities where it is believed pilgrims could sleep and receive visions and healing from the Divine. Here too curse tablets have been found. Nodens was associated with hunting, healing and with the sea[38] and may be 'Node', a sea god recognised by Robert Cochrane's covine, and guardian king of the elemental castle of the west.[39]

The various bounties of the sea have given it magical associations with fertility and abundance. As late as the 18th century, the people of the Isle of Lewis performed nocturnal rites of offering each Hallowe'en to a sea deity; Seonaidh, Shoni or Shoney. Each family would provide a bag of malt which was used to brew a special beer. From this, one chosen from the community would draw a cupful and would, at night, wade out into the sea and call: "Seonaidh, I give thee this cup of ale, hoping that thou wilt be so good as to send us plenty of seaware for enriching our ground during the coming year." After which he would throw the beer into the sea. All would then go to the kirk to hold a silent vigil, until a single candle burning upon the altar had extinguished itself, upon which the people would go into the fields and spend the remainder of the night enjoying the beer with food, singing and dancing. If the rite had been a success, it was believed that Seonaidh would provide the island with plenty of seaweed with which to fertilise the fields, thus resulting in an abundant harvest for the community.[40]

---

37. Ibid, p. 72.
38. Ibid, p. 24.
39. Howard, Michael. *The Master of the Clan, Pagan Dawn* No. 142.
40. Howard, Michael. *Scottish Witches & Warlocks*, p. 14, & wikipedia.org/wiki/Seonaidh

Water & the Witch-Cult

The old witch beliefs or 'witch-cult' of the British Isles, may be said to be bifurcated into two related, and yet quite distinct traditions; the popular beliefs about witches held by the general populace, and the actual practices of witchcraft. In a number of ways, water may be found to hold a role at the heart of both, examples of which we have already encountered.

Within the generally held beliefs about witchcraft, particularly in relation to how its practitioners ought to be dealt with, countered or guarded against, traditions of popular magic were often resorted to, wherein water is again often to be found.

The most infamous of these acts, employed either as a simple act of mob brutality and punishment, or as an act of popular magical divination to 'discover' those suspected of witchcraft, was of course the 'swimming' of witches.

Taken to a river, or perhaps a village pond, the suspected witch would be bound in a particular crosswise fashion; the thumb of the right hand being tied to the toe of the left foot, and the thumb of the left hand tied to the toe of the right foot. A rope might also have been bound about the suspect, allowing men stood on the banks of the water to retrieve their victim, or possibly to feign floating by holding the rope taught with their victim bound at its midst. Before being put into the water, the victim might also be wrapped in a sheet or blanket.[41]

The tradition of determining innocence by the victim's sinking beneath the waters, all too often to drown, or guilt by their floating, had continued in the popular belief from older ordeals of water, and was a practice actively encouraged, although at that time it was technically illegal, by the approval of King James VI of Scotland.[42] In his Daemonologie, published in 1597, the king advocated the practice of 'swimming', and attributed its efficacy in revealing witches, by their floating, to God's pure water rejecting witches who by their deeds had 'shaken off the sacred Water of Baptism, and wilfully refuse the benefit thereof'.

Christina Hole explains that the practice was a debased and crude form of the ancient Northern European 'ordeal by water'; a ceremony via which God was petitioned to reveal innocence or guilt, and involved fasting, prayer and confession, and strict rules for the protection of the accused.[43]

Such ordeals in England were made illegal by Henry III in 1219, however the 'swimmings' continued to be enthusiastically and popularly employed for centuries after, with the authorities often turning a blind eye. However, there were indeed cases where arrests, prosecutions and even executions of those who subjected suspected witches to 'swimming' occurred, particularly where the rite's victim had died as a result.[44]

Whilst the British were quite capable of regarding the figure of the witch with great fear and hatred,

---

41. Gurdon, Eveline Camilla (Ed.). *Old Suffolk Love and Cure Charms*, p.
42. Howard, Michael. *Scottish Witches & Warlocks*, p. 42.
43. Hole, Christina. *Witchcraft in Britain*, p. 77-78.
44. Ibid, p. 171.

Water & the Witch-Cult

and administering ruthless punishments for those suspected of magical ability and 'dealings with the Devil', they seem conversely to have possessed equal capacity for attributing the powers of the witch to adored national heroes.

One such figure is of course Sir Francis Drake, around whom much witch-lore had gathered in his native Devonshire; often featuring the Vice Admiral's magical powers over water.

Drake was regarded as a powerful magician and witch; having sold his soul to the Devil in exchange for his powers and for victory over his enemies, including of course the Armada.[45] It was believed that he possessed familiar spirits and presided as witch-master, or 'Man in Black' over several covens. Under his direction, it is said, his covens raised the storms that devastated part of the Spanish fleet.[46] Other tales are told of Drake's witch-magic against the Armada. Famous is the tale of his game of bowls on Plymouth Hoe, which was continued to its end despite the appearance of the advancing Spanish ships. Upon the game's completion, Drake ordered a huge log of timber and a hatchet to be brought to the Hoe. Over the log he uttered an incantation before chopping it into pieces, each to be thrown into the sea whereupon they transformed into fire-ships and defeated the Armada.[47] At Devil's Point, overlooking Plymouth Sound, Drake is also said to have performed magical rites against the Armada. Here, a legend tells of him whittling a stick, its shavings becoming fully rigged ships as they fell into the sea.[48]

---

45. Howard, Michael. *West Country Witches*, p. 73.
46. Ibid, p. 74.
47. Ibid. & Whitlock, Ralph. *The Folklore of Devon*, p. 72.
48. Ibid.

Another legend of Drake's magical powers concerns his construction of Drake's Leat, via which Plymouth received its first reliable water supply. When he was Mayor of Plymouth, a severe drought hit the town one summer, and so Drake rode up onto Dartmoor in search of a spring. When he found what he was looking for, on Sheepstor, he uttered a magical incantation over the trickling water, causing a stream to arise and burst forth from the rocks. Riding back to Plymouth, the stream followed close behind his horse all the way to the city.[49]

Water & the Witches' Round

By baying dog and moon-beam,
by lantern, stave and upright stone,
Come fathom the starlit heights of Heaven
in the Old Dew-pool of Cain...

ANDREW CHUMBLEY, *Azoetia*

Within both popular belief, and the ways of witchcraft, water has long been associated with spirit presences, spiritual boundaries and a tool of transformation – a washer away of that which is undesired in order to bring forth a new circumstance, and thus a tool of death and rebirth. Just as it is within the rites of clergy and folk-magical practice, within the circles of witchcraft too is water to be found, serving a multiplicity of purposes.

Within rites clerical and folk-magical, a principal purpose of the magical use of water is to cleanse, purify and exorcise, and it is a use to which water may first be put within many a witches' Round.

---

49. Howard, Michael. *West Country Witches*, p. 73, & St. Leger-Gordon, Ruth E. *The Witchcraft and Folklore of Dartmoor*, 33.

The tradition of employing waters for the exorcising of impurity, sin and evil may be found in the Hebrew Bible, Book of Numbers, 19:

> *And a clean person shall take hyssop, and dip it in the water, and sprinkle it upon the tent, and upon all the vessels, and upon the persons that were there, and upon him that touched a bone, or one slain, or one dead, or a grave: And the clean person shall sprinkle upon the unclean on the third day, and on the seventh day: and on the seventh day he shall purify himself, and wash his clothes, and bathe himself in water, and shall be clean at even. But the man that shall be unclean, and shall not purify himself, that soul shall be cut off from among the congregation, because he hath defiled the sanctuary of the LORD: the water of separation hath not been sprinkled upon him; he is unclean.*

Herein we find an assertion of belief that ritual washing and sprinkling with water is a means of spiritual purification and that state of purity is essential for unity with God, for the 'unclean' are 'cut off'. Herein also is found the old tradition of hyssop's employment in such acts, to be encountered also within the Psalms:

> 51:7 *Purge me with hyssop, and I shall be clean: wash me, and I shall be whiter than snow.*

The employment of the hyssop as a ritual aspergillum is of course also to be found within the grimoire tradition, via which, in addition to popular magical usage of the Bible, the practice may have entered into folk-magic and witchcraft.

Within *The Key of Solomon*, the instructions 'Of the water and of the Hyssop', tell of the consecration of the water and the salt, as well as the making and use of the herbal aspergillum. By its use may all items of ritual be exorcised, purified and made sacred via the creative

Wisht Waters

potency of the combined water and salt and the virtue of the herbs:

"Prepare a Censer in the day and hour of Mercury, with the odoriferous Spices of the Art. After this thou shalt take a vessel of brass, of lead varnished within and without, or of earth, which thou shalt fill with most clear spring water, and thou shalt have salt, and say these words over the salt – *Tzabaoth Messiach, Emanuel, Elohim Gibor, Yod He Vau He; O God, Who art the Truth and the Life, deign to bless and sanctify this Creature of Salt, to serve unto us for help, protection, and assistance in this Art, experiment, and operation, and may it be a succour unto us.* – After this cast the salt into the vessel wherein is the Water, and say the following Psalms: CII, LIV, VI, and LXVII.

Thou shalt then make unto thyself a Sprinkler of vervain, fennel, lavender, sage, valerian, mint, garden-basil, rosemary, and hyssop, gathered in the day and hour of Mercury, the moon being in her increase. Bind together these herbs with a thread spun by a young maiden, and engrave upon the handle on the one side the characters shown in Figure 82, and on the other side those given in Figure 83:

After this thou mayest use the Water, using the Sprinkler whenever it is necessary; and know that wheresoever thou shalt sprinkle this Water, it will chase away all Phantoms, and they shall be unable

Water & the Witch-Cult

to hinder or annoy any. With this same Water thou shalt make all the preparations of the Art."[50]

There are of course many influences, or parallels, from this particular grimoire to be found within the rites of the various streams of contemporary Craft.

The consecration of the water and salt are an established feature of the opening of rites within the Craft of Wicca, however its role within the circle, and indeed the role of the circle itself, appear to have been understood differently amongst some of Wicca's elder practitioners. Gerald Gardner appears to have had a particular dislike, or fear of spirits; for within the writings of Cecil Williamson, held within the Museum of Witchcraft's archives, we find tales of Gardner fleeing in terror from the scene where censers performed in such away that the arising smoke they produced took forms uncannily suggestive of spirit manifestation. Cecil also tells of Gardner's apparent disinterest in the idea of the familiar spirit; a concept deeply engrained within witchcraft tradition, yet strangely absent from Gardner's vision of the Craft.

To Gerald Gardner then, the idea that the witches' circle provided a barrier against the intrusion of spirits, and that this function may be greatly enhanced by ritual exorcism via consecrated water and salt, might have been very attractive.

One of Gardner's High Priestesses apparently insisted however; "A circle is drawn to contain and concentrate the power raised by witches, not to keep evil spirits out: spirits, evil or otherwise, have no part in witch rituals.".[51]

Within many Craft streams, however, it may be said that spirits certainly do have a role within witch rites,

---

50. *Of the Water and of the Hyssop, The Key of Solomon*, various editions.
51. Holzer, Hans. *Encyclopedia of Witchcraft & Demonology*, p. 106.

and other adherents of the Wiccan Craft have viewed the consecration of the circle and its exorcism as both a preparation of a space, blessed, purified and set apart for sacred acts before the presence of the Divine, as well a banishing and protection from evil influences.

In *The Devil's Prayerbook* – an interesting version of *The Book of Shadows* and early disclosure of Wiccan ritual – these sentiments are to be found in the wording for the rite of 'Invocation and Consecration of the Circle';

> *Be this salt dedicated to the Lord and the Lady to keep us from evil and to protect us in this time. Be this water dedicated to the Lord and the Lady to keep us from peril and to purify this place.*

The water and salt are then mixed and sprinkled sunwise around the circle with the words;

> *May we cast from us all evil and darkness, viciousness and malice. May we become that which we must be before the Lord and the Lady, seeking ill to no one. May we be clean within and without that we are acceptable before them.*[52]

Within the various streams of modern traditional Craft, the consecration of water and salt are also to be found within the preparation of the circle and ritual objects.

The themes of exorcism, purification and the sacred are again present, although, there may be an emphasis on water's conflux with the other elements in Quintessence. Herein the essences of creation are employed in unison to exorcise and 'rebirth' the manifest item or place unto sacred purpose, free of intrusion or unwanted influence.

In Paul Huson's ground breaking and much maligned *Mastering Witchcraft*, we find the ritual employment of water in such a manner;

---

52. Witch, A. *The Devil's Prayerbook*, 43.

> *The salt, water, and incense stand for the four elements of the Wise – earth, water, and fire, together with air – symbolically constituting the basis of the material universe... By exorcising anything, you are in effect symbolically using these four basic constituents to "wash" the article of all extraneous vibrations, prior to recharging it with your own will and concentrated witch power.*[53]

Within Huson's Exorcism by Salt, Water and Incense, a small pinch of new salt is cast into a bowl of fresh water, over which the practitioner breathes these words onto the water's surface; 'Water and earth where you are cast no spell nor adverse purpose last not in complete accord with me. As my word, so mote it be!'[54]

For the consecration of ritual items, water is employed in this manner, but also as a conduit for the virtues of certain herbs. Under a waxing moon, the consecration of the cup and thurible involves vervain, mint, basil, rosemary, hyssop, lavender, sage, valerian and fennel being steeped within the salt water. The item is sprinkled with the water and passed through the incense smoke with the words; 'By water and fire I conjure thee that there remain within thy frame no adverse thought nor enmity. Hear my will! Attend to me! As my word, so mote it be!'[55]

In consecrating the athame, the manner of water's employment is most fitting to the nature of the tool, wherein the blade is thrice tempered, after heating in burning coals, within an infusion of martial herbs to which a few drops of the witch's blood, or that of a black cat, have been added.[56] Calling to mind the forge of the

---

53. Huson, Paul. *Mastering Witchcraft*, p. 49-50.
54. Ibid.
55. Ibid, p. 52-54.
56. Ibid, p. 54-55.

magician-blacksmith and Tubal Cain, the rite is potently symbolic of the creative act, the union in Quintessence of above and below forming the 'all potential' from which that which is desired may be born forth under the directorship of the witch's will; of which the athame is emblematic.

Within the circles of the 'Old Craft' we may find the enshrinement and very embodiment of Quintessence, 'one pointedness' and 'All is One' as a tenet literally central to various streams of traditional witchcraft.

In Quintessence is the union of all, thus all that is manifest; the mundane elements of creation, and the spiritual elements of being, conjoin and have their source in Quintessence. It is the primordial source of creation, power and all-gnosis, thus 'magical Quintessence' may be said to be the realisation that 'All is One', and the attainment of consciousness of one's connection to all via the pure spring from which all magic flows forth, pervading all that is.

It is a tenet of which the witches' circle is itself emblematic, via its eternal encompassment of the Ways crossing as One at its axial midst.

The elements all are employed often within the circle's consecration via the common practice of sprinkling the perimeter, or to the quarters, with the blessed water, co-mixed in creative union with the salt of life, followed by censing as the thurible issues forth the sweet fumes of resins and wort; their virtues released by the coals of fire.

Within the rites of many traditions are the elemental virtues then to be convoked to their union at the circle's centre, where we may find them together enciphered in the fire heating the aqueous content of the earthly body of the witch's cauldron, to send forth its virtuous vapors unto the airy heights.

Here, the fluids of the cauldron, the witches' vessel of arte, may be seen to be the focal-point of the operations of the circle; being the medium into which are placed the materia-magica of the Work, to bring about banishment in the vessel's leftward stirring, or in rightward conjuration for the birthing forth of that which is desired.

The central fluids of the cauldron, their empowerment by Quintessential union and symbolic creative act, and the dispersing of their potent virtues in fecund consecration unto the circle of arte, are exemplified in the rites of Cochrane's covine;

> *The ritual proper began with the men pacing around the fire, chanting and plunging their knives into the cauldron. Then the women elevated a platter (symbolising the Grail) and dipped it into the liquid. A sword was then plunged in the boiling cauldron and the liquid was scattered to the four quarters using its blade.*[57]

Each Way of the elements is a path unto Quintessence, from whence their power flows through all manifestation, yet the element of water may be seen to be possessed of an especial 'closeness' to Quintessence.

It is the Way of water that invites us to tread backward the spiraling path of inward return; for it is irresistibly the element of memory, the primordial and amniotic sea of the depths mirroring the heavenly sea of stars. Whilst water is also of the river that divides the quick and the dead, washing away memory as life passes into death and again into life, it is the element of omniscience for water takes on and retains all that is washed within it;

> *The waters of the sea will give you patience, omninesence, since the Sea is a womb that contains a memory of all things.*[58]

---

57. Howard, Michael. *The Master of the Clan*, Pagan Dawn No. 142.
58. Robert Cochrane, writing to Joe Wilson, 1966.

To the Arte Magical we find part of water's central significance; like the fire kindled at the centre of the witches' circle – the light of creation arising from the progenitrix of primordial chaos, water too is emblematic of all-potentiality; for it is 'fons et origo, the source of all possible existence'.[59]

It is this virtue which is imparted upon the circle, and partaken of by all who enter it, in its asperging, preparing the ritual ground, and its participants for the Divine presence and the creative work of magic, immersed in the source of its power.

The meeting of the Ways and the Quintessential source of power is named in some witch traditions as the Castle. Sometimes it is situated at the centre of the circle, sometimes it is the circle itself, and there may be a Castle of the elements to each quarter.

Within the context of witch rites, Evan John Jones described the centrally situated Castle thus;

> *four square castle of the winds with a gateway set in the middle of each wall. ...Where the four lines intersect is the symbolic source of all power. The spot where the natural world meets the world of the supernatural, thus becoming the gateway through which the power flows. ...As well as being considered the place where the natural and supernatural meet, it is also symbolic of the unnamed Goddess, the pro-genetrix of all Creation. The place where order started to develop from chaos, thus giving form to the preordained universe we live in and whose mysteries we are still discovering.*[60]

Herein, water's traditional attribution as a boundary between the worlds of the quick and the dead have significance within witch rites, for the Castle is reached by the crossing of water.

---

59. Éliade, Mircéa. *Patterns in Comparative Religion*, p. 188.
60. Jones, Evan John. *The Ritual of the Castle, The Cauldron* No. 79.

Within 'The Ritual of the Castle', Evan John Jones explains that 'it is over water that our soul has to go to reach the island and the Castle that will be its resting place until rebirth.'

The circle is composed for this rite of three rings; the first and outer ring represents life, and is cast with salt, the next ring is representative of death and eventual rebirth and is cast of the ashes of willow and birch. The last and inner ring is the River and is cast of water, wine, vinegar and salt. Herein are represented Time and the river boundary between the worlds of the living and of spirit, in wine are the joys of life represented, and in the vinegar and salt the sadness of life, both washed away in the waters of oblivion as one passes between life and death. The Castle, inhabiting the centre, is encompassed by the River, and the states of life and death one must pass through in order to cross its waters and return to the Castle and the Cauldron of Creation; 'potent with infinite possibilities'.

The waters that form the boundary between the quick and the dead are invoked within Andrew Chumbley's Exorcism of Water within the *Azoëtia*:

> *O' Creature of Water!*
> *Be ye potent as the Stygian Divide,*
> *whereby all Gods are sworn and bound in Oath.*
> *Feign ye the Blood of all slain in Worship.*
> *Be ye free from all Taint and Uncleanliness,*
> *and be ye Pure unto the One Spirit.*

Potently thematic of passage between the worlds, purification, the creative act and the unity of the elements in Quintessence is the employment within the circle of the broom. That the broom is a Craft emblem of spirit flight between the worlds is obvious, as is the symbolic creative union of the masculine shaft with the feminine brush, and the tool's mundane uses to sweep clear. It is emblematic of Quintessence by virtue of its material components; the shaft of ash and the brush of birch bound by willow; representing respectively air/spirit, earth and water. Within the magico-sexual ecstatic spirit flight, brought on by the *unguentum sabbati* and applied via the ashen shaft, we have the element of fire.

The situation of the watery willow binding at the centre of the broom is entirely apposite to the tool's use, within some Craft streams, as the 'bridge' via which to enter the circle. Here the broom may be positioned slightly diagonally across the circle's edge, at the chosen point of ingress. The earthly brush of birch outside the circle, the watery willow binding upon the circle's perimeter, and the shaft of airy spirit ash within the circle; all combine to represent a passing from the world of the quick into the spirit world, or from the everyday state of being into sacred and numinous space as the witch steps across the 'broom-bridge' into the circle of arte where water is the threshold.

It is fitting that, in some streams of Craft, the circle may be sprinkled by consecrated water thrown from the brush of the broom; an act redolent with symbolism of fertility, exorcism/purification, passage into the Otherworld and the power of Quintessence. The circle itself becomes as the sacred pool; the well of wisdom and the cauldron of transformation and all-potential.

In considering water's symbolism as the boundary between the quick and the dead, and a veil unto the world of spirit, we see, of course, that the element is ascribed in many Craft traditions unto the western quarter of the circle. It is the direction of rest and repose, and that which receives the sun into the Underworld following its fiery birth from the east. A direction of liminality; a theme common within the magical lore of water, it is the direction of the magical time of dusk, and the autumnal tide betwixt summer and winter through which the round of the year journeys from light and life into death and the dark time. Evan John Jones ascribes the sacrificial Old Horned God as the guardian of the west:

> *Like the setting sun itself, his powers are waning with the onset of old age, and all he has left is the waiting for the end and the memories of the past. Thus youth is counter-balanced by old age or, to put it another way, fire by water.*[61]

The psychopompic, twilight nature of the water element, and its ascribed quarter within the witches' circle is exemplified beautifully within the *Azoëtia* via Andrew Chumbley's conjuration of the west:

> *Ye Lords of the Western Watchtower!*
> *Ye Grey Gods of Twilight,*
> *Ye Mighty Ones that guard the Dusk,*
> *Ye Sovereign Spirits of Zephyrus,*
> *Ye Spirits of the Western Wind*
> *and all ye Spirits of the Water,*
> *I do call, I do rouse, I do summon you here,*
> *To witness, to bind and to guard this Rite.*
> *Watcher of the West!*
> *By the Sign and the Word of the Fivefold Star,*
> *I charge Thee!*

---

61. Jones, Evan John. *The Ritual of the Castle, The Cauldron* No. 79.

~ Communion & the Cauldron-Cup ~

*...By the Moon Above in the Water Below,
By the Devil's Wine, and the Bread of Hosts,
So Mote it Be!*[62]

Aqueous symbolism, the creative act and imbibing of the numinous arise again within the Craft via the witch rites of communion.

Such rites operate around the *foci* of the cauldron and cup; 'the magical vessel of spiritual nourishment and omniscience, the well in which the dead are restored to life. The witch's cauldron is a psychic crucible in which the essences of consciousness are subtly fermented and distilled.'[63]

The witch's cauldron as a magical crucible of birth, death and rebirth, Divine inspiration and transformation has a truly ancient presence within magical folklore. The Cauldron of Ceridwen is steeped in aqueous mystery; its legend involving a submerged city, and a magical lake in which dwelt the witch Ceridwen in serpentine form. Skilled in the magical lore of plants, she prepared for her dark son Morfan a cauldron of inspiration. Within her magical vessel, for a whole year and one day, the herbs alkanet, cowslip, dandelion, herb-bennet, marsh-cinquefoil, mayweed, stitchwort, wild-pansy and wood-sorrell, had to be placed to boil in order to produce just three precious drops of the Awen of Divine inspiration. Imparted unto those who imbibed of the magical elixir, would be the skills of the bard, omniscience and the gift of foresight. All did not go according to Ceridwen's plan, for the cauldron cracked, its remaining liquid became

---

62. Schulke, Daniel A. *The Blood Compact of the Witching Cup.*
63. Jackson, Nigel. *Call of the Horned Piper*, p. 34.

poisonous, ran into a stream and made the land sterile. Gwion, who consumed the cauldron's Awen instead of Ceridwen's son Morfan was in turn consumed in the form of grain by Ceridwen in their shape-shifting chase. Ceridwen later gives re-birth to him and gives the child up to fate by setting him afloat in a coracle to later be discovered and named Taliesin. Within the old legend we may find initiatory themes of death, entry into the Underworld, leading to rebirth via the cauldron/womb of the goddess.[64] Herein we may also find intimations of the rebirth of the Divine 'Star Child' bearing forth illumination from the dark.

The power of the cauldron to transform death unto rebirth is present also within the legend of the Cauldron of Bran, from which those killed in battle would emerge restored unto life, after having been immersed within its waters the previous day.[65]

Initiatory themes of Divine inspiration and omniscience are to be found also within the Norse legend of the Midguard well, entirely cognate in magical lore with the cauldron's sacred waters, guarded by the Wise One Mimir. Unto the one who drank of its waters, this sacred spring would impart the gift of All-Knowledge. Woden desired to drink of the wisdom of the waters, but in doing so had to pay Mimir with one of his own eyes.[66]

The cauldron's employment within the witch rites of communion are treated within the writings of Cochrane/Bowers, wherein we find that the Divine inspiration of the cauldron was activated by the creative act of 'the sacred marriage' via the thrusting of the spear into its depths; a union of spirit within matter by which the

---

64. Howard, Michael. *Welsh Witches and Wizards*, p. 13-26.
65. Whelan, Edna. *The Magic and Mystery of Holy Wells*, p. 67.
66. Ibid, p. 86.

liquids of the cauldron are transformed into the Aqua Vitae – the waters of life, there to be imbibed of by the witch-congregation; a partaking of 'inspiration or spirit brought to earth.'[67]

The act is described by Bowers as 'literally drawing down the Moon'. We learn from Michael Howard, writing of the activities of Bowers' covine, that the rite of communion at the full of the moon might involve a unique version of 'drawing down the moon' by use of a small mirror – an item regarded within the circle as a 'doorway into the astral realms, and macro-cosmic reflector of virtue. Gateway of ingress and egress.'[68]

Into the wine-filled cup, the Lady would reflect the light of the moon, by careful positioning of the mirror as the covine paced the mill nine times about her. The Magister approached, bearing in his right hand the blade and a lit lantern in his left. The blade was sharpened upon the whetstone before being plunged into the wine; stirring it thrice. The virtues of the cup's transformed content were then imparted unto the circle, upon the blade's withdrawal, from which the wine would be splashed to the four quarters before its imbibing from the cup by the covine.[69]

The moon, a mirror itself of the sun, brings the double light to dance upon the liquid's surface in its transformation by the creative act, there to be partaken of by those who imbibe of the 'Wines of the Sabbat, the conjoined elixirs of Sun and Moon made manifest and married according to their secret orbits, conjunctions and alignments in the Flesh of the Priests and Priestesses of Arte.'[70]

---

67. Robert Cochrane writing to Joe Wilson.
68. Oates, Shani. *Tubelo's Green Fire*, p. 238.
69. Howard, Michael. *The Master of the Clan*, Pagan Dawn No. 142
70. Chumbley, Andrew. *The Azoëtia*.

Water & the Witch-Cult

Cecil Williamson tells us that 'calling down the moon' was a rite performed by the 'sea witches' of Devon and Cornwall in order to gain wisdom. He describes the practice as 'a form of self hypnosis or mesmerism'. To call down the moon, the witch is to go to a high cliff top, granting a clear view of the full moon reflected in the sea. Those who have observed the full moon in such a way will be familiar with the 'silver path' extending towards oneself across the waters. Here the witch will sit and gaze directly at the moon, and then draw her gaze to follow the silver path towards her until it disappears beneath the cliff's edge. The repetition of this act, Cecil explains, will cause the moon to appear 'like a vast balloon', right in front of one. Within the sphere will be contained a 'swirling mass of vapour' from which a large human face will form to gaze back into the eyes of the witch. With this manifestation, the sea witch can hold a productive conversation, before it gently drifts away 'with a slight wobble and then all of a sudden with a great blast of air - whoosh, and it shoots off and is gone in an instant'.[71]

Within J. W. Brodie-Innes' intriguing 1915 book 'The Devil's Mistress', we find what appears to be another unique version of 'drawing down the moon', again involving water, seemingly for initiatory purposes. We are told by Brodie-Innes that 'The Devil's Mistress' is a dramatic telling of the life of the Scottish Witch Isabel Goudie, vouched by contemporary writings and her own story 'preserved in the archives in the Justiciary Court in Edinburgh'. Within the book we read of Goudie's ritual preparation of 'moon paste', by which she will have the power to 'bring together parted lovers' and lift the sicknesses that 'are the result of the ill-will of some witch'. Also, by the solitary rite, her 'beauty will

---

71. Williamson, Cecil. Description of Museum of Witchcraft item No. 137.

be far beyond the beauty of mortal women' and it will win her 'the power that would make her more than a queen, almost the secret arbiter of destiny to all the countryside'.

The rite requires that the witch gathers water from seven wells, at each of which she must overcome the 'guardian demon' who watches over the virtue of the waters. When the waters are drawn, they must be blessed in the name of Hecate before the door to kirks and chapels nearby, and used to anoint the brow.

The story tells us that, after doing this, at sunset the next day Goudie mixed certain prescribed herbs, pounding them together, before kneading clay taken 'from a special place' which was then dried over the fire, pounded 'fine like meal', and mixed it with the herbs before being pounded again and put into an iron pot.

Goudie then took the ewer of well waters, the iron pot and a kneading trough covered with dark green plaid to Aulderne kirkyard. Here she emptied into the trough the powdered clay and herbs and looked up to the moon. She poured the waters from the ewer into the trough, and kneaded the clay into a thin paste. Retiring to the north-east corner of the kirkyard, she loosened and let slip her gowns, raised her arms in supplication to the moon, and moved forward towards the trough beginning her chant to Lucina. Within the trough, she saw the moon reflected in the surface of the clay-water, and around it she circumambulated widdershins, to the south-east. Here she faced the trough, the moon behind her. She pressed the backs of her hands against her shoulders, threw her head backwards as far as she could and lifted her eyes until the moon came into view. Once more round widdershins until she faced again the south and saw the moon reflected in the trough. Here she chanted the second part of her triple invocation; to Diana. Goudie turned again, leaning backwards to see the moon, and came to the north of the trough where the moon shone directly behind it. Here lifting her arms to the moon, she chanted the third part of her invocation; to Hecate. Moving now towards the moon, she stumbled towards the trough, stopping so she could see the moons reflection within it and raised her eyes again to the moon's face in the sky. Here she experienced 'a simulacrum as it were of the moon detaching itself from the luminary and floating downwards, pale and ghostlike, as though to join the image of itself in the trough'. This reflection grew brighter as the moon itself in the heaven seemed to grow dim 'as though only the spectre of itself remained'. A mist arose from the trough around the brilliant orb, the water seemed to boil and white churning foam formed on its surface. With her hands she gathered up the foam as it boiled over, throwing it into the plaid until all was gone. Behind the trough, looking at her, stood a 'wondrous beautiful female form, pale and silvery', she was 'fully twice the size and height of common humanity'. The form embraced her and 'the weariness vanished and it was as though a new vigorous life was poured into her'. Opening her eyes, the dark master stood smiling beside her, for she was now worthy to be his bride and queen of the coven.[72]

A far simpler solitary rite of witch initiation, also involving water and the moon, was employed in Shetland. Here, at midnight and under a full moon, one had to venture forth to a beach; a place of magical liminality. Here is then employed the familiar formula of crouching to place the left hand beneath the left foot, and the right hand upon the head with the spoken charm: "The mighty master Devil take what is between these my two hands". The completion of this rite would impart upon the new witch the power over land, sea and the 'elemental forces of earth and water'.[73]

---

72. Brodie-Innes, J.W. *The Devil's Mistress*, p. 123-141.

73. Howard, Michael. *Scottish Witches & Warlocks*, p. 27.

Wisht Waters

Another solitary initiatory rite requiring the virtues of water and the moon, and of most notoriety in its various forms, is of course the rite of the 'Toad Bone'.

Within his thorough treatise of the tradition, Andrew Chumbley relates in 'The Leaper Between' the varying manifestations of the rite, each employing water as the very catalyst and actuating force for the famed powers of the toad bone amulet. The methodology of the rite, as employed by folk magicians, witches, and amongst the brethren of the Society of the Horseman's Word, generally follows a pattern deviated from only in minor details.

The flesh is flensed from the body of the toad, which has sometimes been put to death by sacrifice upon the thorn, often by the action of ants. The unveiled bones are then to be gathered, and taken upon a clear night of the full moon to a flowing stream in which the moon's image is reflected. Therein shall the bones be cast; the waters revealing unto the initiate the bone of power.

The talismanic bone may indicate itself by turning and flowing against the current of the stream, thus turning against the natural or common order of things. Some say that the stream employed for the rite must be one that flows from the north to the south.[74] The uncanny bone may also announce itself by screaming, just as the potent mandrake is said to do upon being pulled from the earth. Andrew Chumbley relates that, in the very moment the toad-witch draws forth the bone of power from the moon-silvered waters, all of nature shall then turn against them, signalling the approaching of the power.

We are told also that if a stream has been 'consecrated' by its use by one to pass through the ordeals of the toad rite, stones may be drawn from it and passed on to others of the Path to be used in the manner of the Sabbatic Coin, in lieu of the toad-bone.

---

74. Pennick, Nigel. *Operative Witchcraft*, p. 96.

In North Pembrokeshire, Toadmen would perform the rite at Caman Brook; a liminal boundary of Nevern Church's graveyard. The revealed bone would be taken and carried within the pocket for three days and three nights. Each midnight, the would-be Toadman would venture to Trellyffant; a Neolithic burial chamber whose name means 'Toad's Town'. Here the ancient stones would be circumambulated thrice against the sun, upon the completion of which, the Devil was said to appear, and challenge the practitioner for the bone. If the practitioner succeeded in retaining the bone, he was thereafter an empowered Toadman, and possessed of the ability to charm animals, especially horses.[75]

Andrew Chumbley wrote of a variation of the rite, published in Norfolk in 1835. In this method, the usual formula is followed up to the casting of the bones into the stream. However, it appears that all of the bones were then retrieved, later to be ground into a powder. This would impart the power to jade a horse by touching him on the shoulder, or on the rump to draw him.

Whilst it would appear that the rite of the toad bone was undertaken by male folk-magicians, particularly so within the all male secret society of the Horsemen, knowledge of the rite was possessed and put into use by women. The 18th century Huntingtoft wise woman, Tilly Baldry, performed the rite by catching a 'hoppin' toad' and carrying it between her breasts until it putrefied 'to the back-boon'. This was then taken to a stream at midnight and held over the flowing waters until the Devil appeared and pulled her over the water. Upon this crossing of the liminal waters by the hand of the Devil, Tilly was made a witch.

Within Reginald Scot's 1584 Discoverie of Witchcraft, the toad bone rite is present, yet the bones of virtue are those that sink upon being cast into water. These

---

75. Howard, Michael. *Welsh Witches and Wizards*, p. 54.

are taken up and kept within a bag of white linen, and may cause love in a woman, but excite hate within a man touched by them

Andrew Chumbley also highlights the rite in Indian magical tradition, recorded in 1907. Here, the exhumed bones of a frog, after having been buried for seven days, would be cast into water. The bones that sank beneath the surface possessed the power to excite hatred, whilst those that floated could be employed to bring about love. We find within these rites potent themes, such as the power of the moon above mirrored in the waters below (a 'drawing down' of illumination from the heavens unto the depths), the power of liminal boundaries and times, and initiatory encounters with the Devil. The bone, which may be revealed by its turning against natural order, imparts the ability to invert states of being, to transform hate into love, stubborn or wild animals into passive compliancy or vice versa. The magical toad bone is thus an amulet of 'turning'.

The creature of the toad is one so intimate to the lore of folk-magic and witchery, perhaps for its liminal nature, which it shares of course with water itself. Passing upon land, beneath the earth, or beneath the waters, the toad is seen in the magical mind to cross the boundaries between the worlds, it is thus of interest that toads were employed within some recipes for 'flying ointment" affording the witch such free passage between the worlds.[76]

A creature so chthonic in nature, its mysteries are shrouded in the night mists of the unknown. To recognise such power in the 'lowly' toad is to have knowledge of the unity of power and the Divine light inherent in and pervading all from the heights to the depths.

---

76. Jackson, Nigel. *Call of the Horned Piper*, p. 43.

Bibliography

Baring-Gould, Sabine and Fisher, John. *The Lives of the British Saints* Volume 4 (London 1907)

Bord, Janet & Colin. *Sacred Waters* (Paladin 1986)

Bord, Janet. *Cures and Curses – Ritual and Cult at Holy Wells* (Heart of Albion 2006)

Bottrell, William. *Traditions and Hearthside Stories of West Cornwall* (1870)

Brodie-Innes, J.W. *The Devil's Mistress* (Ramble House 2006)

Buckland, Raymond. *Gypsy Witchcraft and Magic* (Llewellyn 1998)

Cadbury, Tabitha. *The Clarke Collection of Charms and Amulets* (Museum of Witchcraft Archive)

Caple, John and Leyshon, Nell. *Somerset – The Paintings of John Caple* (White Lane Press 2007)

Chumbley, Andrew. *ONE: The Grimoire of the Golden Toad* (Xoanon 2000)
   Azoëtia (Xoanon 2002)
   The Leaper Between (Three Hands Press 2012)

Cooke, Ian. *Mermaid to Merrymaid – Journey to the Stones* (Men-an-Tol Studio 1987)

Courtney, M. A. *Cornish Feasts and Folklore* (EP 1973)

Bibliography

Courtney, R.A. *Cornwall's Holy Wells – Their Pagan Origins* (Oakmagic 1997)

de Givry, Grillot. *Witchcraft: Magic and Alchemy (Houghton Mifflin* 1931 / Dover Publications 1971)

Éliade, Mircéa. *Patterns in Comparative Religion* (Sheed and Ward, 1979)

Farquharson-Coe, A. *Devon's Witchcraft* (James Pike 1975)

Glass, Justine. *Witchcraft, The Sixth Sense – And Us* (Neville Spearman 1965)

Gurdon, Eveline Camilla (Ed.). *Old Suffolk Love and Cure Charms* (Oakmagic 2005)

Harland, John. Wilkinson, T.T. *Lancashire Witchcraft Charms and Spells* (Oakmagic 2002)

Henderson, William. *Witchcraft, Toadlore and Charms of the Northern Counties* (Oakmagic 2001)

Hole, Christina. *Witchcraft in Britain* (Granada 1979)

Holzer, Hans. *Encyclopedia of Witchcraft & Demonology* (Octopus 1974)

Howard, Michael. *By Standing Stone and Holy Well* (The Cauldron No. 137)
   Scottish Witches & Warlocks (Three Hands Press 2013)
   The Cauldron of Ceridwen (The Cauldron No. 134)
   The Cunning Man (The Cauldron No.95)
   The Master of the Clan (Pagan Dawn No. 142)
   Welsh Witches and Wizards (Three Hands Press 2009)
   West Country Witches (Three Hands Press 2010)

Hunt, Robert. *Popular Romances of the West of England* (Chatto & Windus 1908)

Huson, Paul. *Mastering Witchcraft* (Putnam 1970)

Jackson, Nigel. *Call of the Horned Piper* (Capall Bann 1994)

Johnson, Nicholas. Rose, Peter. *Cornwall's Archaeological Heritage* (Twelveheads Press 1990)

Jones, Evan John. *The Ritual of the Castle* (The Cauldron No. 79)

Kemp, Gillian. *The Good Spell Book* (Orion 2012)

Latimer, Simon. *Witchcraft and Magic in London* (The Cauldron No. 134)

Lewis, Gareth. *The Faery Doctors* (The Cauldron No. 103)

Mullins, Rose. *White Witches – A Study of Charmers* (PR Publishing)

Oates, Shani. *Tubelo's Green Fire* (Mandrake 2010)

Pennick, Nigel. *Operative Witchcraft* (Lear 2011)

Pickering, David. *Dictionary of Witchcraft* (Brockhampton Press 1996)

Poole, Charles Henry. *Witchcraft Customs and Superstitions of Somerset* (Oakleaf 2001)

Quiller-Couch, Thomas. *Ancient and Holy Wells of Cornwall* (C.J. Clark 1894)

Bibliography

Schulke, Daniel A. *Ars Philtron* (Xoanon 2001)

St. Leger-Gordon, Ruth E. *The Witchcraft and Folklore of Dartmoor* (Hale 1965)

Straffon, Cheryl. *Ancient Sites in West Penwith* (Meyn Mamvro 1992)
Fentynyow Kernow – In Search of Cornwall's Holy Wells (Meyn Mamvro 1998)
Pagan Cornwall – Land of the Goddess (Meyn Mamvro 2012)

Trevelyan, Marie. *Welsh Witchcraft, Charms and Spells* (Oakmagic 1999)

Walker, Charles. *The Encyclopedia of Secret Knowledge* (Limited Editions 1995)

Whelan, Edna. *The Magic and Mystery of Holy Wells* (Capall Bann 2001)

Whitlock, Ralph. *The Folklore of Devon* (B.T. Batsford 1977)

Williamson, Cecil. *Dew Ponds, Moon-Raking & The Ritual of the Shroud* (The Cauldron No. 76)
Notes on Witchcraft (The Museum of Witchcraft Research Archive)

Witch, A. *The Devil's Prayerbook* (Rigel Press 1974)